Unit 2

Christianity:
Ethics

Sheila Butler

Philip Allan Updates, an imprint of Hodder Education, an Hachette UK company, Market Place, Deddington, Oxfordshire OX15 0SE

Orders
Bookpoint Ltd, 130 Milton Park, Abingdon, Oxfordshire OX14 4SB
tel: 01235 827827
fax: 01235 400401
e-mail: education@bookpoint.co.uk
Lines are open 9.00 a.m.–5.00 p.m., Monday to Saturday, with a 24-hour message answering service. You can also order through the Philip Allan Updates website: www.philipallan.co.uk

© Philip Allan Updates 2009
ISBN 978-1-4441-0079-2

First printed 2009
Impression number   5   4   3   2
Year   2014   2013   2012   2011

Illustrations: Jim Watson
Printed in Italy

Hachette UK's policy is to use papers that are natural, renewable and recyclable products and made from wood grown in sustainable forests. The logging and manufacturing processes are expected to conform to the environmental regulations of the country of origin.

Contents

About this book 4

Topic 1
The right to life

Abortion 6

Euthanasia 13

Topic 2
The use of medical technology

Fertility treatments 18

Genetic engineering 23

Cloning 28

Topic 3
Personal responsibility

Sexual relationships 33

Drugs 39

Topic 4
Social responsibility

Marriage 44

Prejudice and discrimination 51

Topic 5
Global concerns

The environment 55

World poverty 60

Topic 6
Conflict

War and peace 67

Crime and punishment 74

Key word index 80

About this book

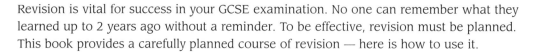

Revision is vital for success in your GCSE examination. No one can remember what they learned up to 2 years ago without a reminder. To be effective, revision must be planned. This book provides a carefully planned course of revision — here is how to use it.

The book	*The route to success*
Contents list	**Step 1** Check which topics you need to revise for your examination. Mark them clearly on the contents list and make sure you revise them.
Revision notes	**Step 2** Each section of the book gives you the facts you need to know for a topic. Read the notes carefully, and list the main points.
Key words	**Step 3** Key words are highlighted in the text and displayed in key word boxes. Learn them and their meanings. They must be used correctly in the examination.
Case study	**Step 4** Each section has a case study. Learn one for each topic. You could do this by listing the main headings with key facts beneath them on a set of revision cards. If your teacher has taught different case studies, use the one you find easiest to remember.
Test yourself	**Step 5** A set of brief questions is given at the end of each section. Answer these to test how much you know. If you get one wrong, revise it again. You can try the questions before you start the topic to check what you know.
Examination questions	**Step 6** Examples of questions are given for you to practise. The more questions you practise, the better you will become at answering them.
Exam tips	**Step 7** The exam tips offer advice for achieving success. Read them and act on the advice when you answer the question.
Key word index	**Step 8** On page 80 there is a list of all the key words and the pages on which they appear. Use this index to check whether you know all the key words. This will help you to decide what you need to look at again.

Command words

All examination questions include **command** or **action** words. These tell you what the examiner wants you to do. Here are two of the most common ones:

- **Describe** — requires detail. For example, you may be asked to describe the work of hospices. Description does not require explanation.
- **Explain** — here the examiner is expecting you to show understanding by giving reasons. For example, you may be asked to explain why many Christians support the hospice movement.

The checklists and advice opposite will help you to prepare for the exam and to make sure you do justice to yourself on the day.

Revision rules

- Start early.

- Plan your time by making a timetable.

- Be realistic — don't try to do too much each night.

- Find somewhere quiet to work.

- Revise thoroughly, including learning the set texts — reading on its own is not enough.

- Summarise your notes, make headings for each topic.

- Ask someone to test you.

- Try to answer some questions from old papers. Your teacher will help you.

If there is anything you don't understand — ask your teacher.

Be prepared

The night before the exam

- Complete your final revision.

- Check the time and place of your examination.

- Get your pens ready.

- Go to bed early and set the alarm clock.

On the examination day

- Don't rush.

- Double check the time and place of your exam and your equipment.

- Arrive early.

- Keep calm — breathe deeply.

- Be positive.

Do you know?

- The exam board setting your paper?

- How many papers you will be taking?

- The date, time and place of each paper?

- How long each paper will be?

- What the subject of each paper will be?

- What the paper will look like? Do you write your answer on the paper or in a separate booklet?

- How many questions you should answer?

- Whether there is a choice of questions?

- Whether any part of the paper is compulsory?

If you don't know the answer to any of these questions as the exam approaches — ask your teacher.

Examination tips

- Keep calm and concentrate.

- Read the paper through before you start to write.

- In Part B, decide which question you are going to answer.

- Make sure you can do all parts of the questions you choose.

- Complete all the questions.

- Don't spend too long on one question at the expense of the others.

- Read each question carefully, then stick to the point and answer questions fully.

- In evaluation questions, include Christian teaching and more than one viewpoint.

- Use all your time.

- Check your answers.

- Do your best.

Topic 1
The right to life

Abortion

Abortion is the deliberate termination of pregnancy. It is permitted under UK law, provided certain conditions are met. The cut-off point for most abortions is 24 weeks.

UK law

Risk to physical health of woman

Selective reduction of foetuses in multiple pregnancy

Risk to physical health of existing children

Risk to mental health of woman

Up to 24 weeks

Risk to mental health of existing children

Legal grounds for abortion

Probability of grave permanent injury to woman's physical health

Up to term

Substantial risk of severe physical disability in foetus

Probability of grave permanent injury to woman's mental health

Risk to life of woman

Substantial risk of severe mental disability in foetus

Secular arguments for and against abortion

For	Against
No child should be unwanted	No child need be unwanted — there are alternatives to abortion
The **embryo/foetus** is just a clump of cells — it is at best a potential life	Life begins at **conception**, when something totally and uniquely new comes into being
A young girl is not ready for the responsibilities of motherhood	A young girl is not mature enough to deal with any long-lasting guilt feelings after abortion
It is cruel to make a raped woman go through with pregnancy	It is wrong to punish a child for the father's action
Aborting a disabled foetus is in the best interests of everyone	It is wrong for those without disability to make quality of life judgements about people with disability
The right to **autonomy** — the mother has the right to choose for herself	The right to autonomy should be limited as in this case the mother is making choices for someone else (the foetus)
The woman knows what is best for herself and the foetus	The woman's emotional state may cloud her judgement

Pro-choice

■ Maternal rights come first

■ She is more fully alive than a foetus

■ She should decide what happens in and to her body

Pro-life

■ Foetal rights come first

■ The foetus is fully alive as a human being with potential

■ The foetus is vulnerable and needs protection

Neil Bromhall/SPL

A 5-month old foetus in the womb

When does life begin?

Biological life begins with the fertilisation of the egg by the sperm, but what is meant here is at what stage is it meaningful life, i.e. life with rights? There are different views on this:

- At conception
  - the **pro-life** view taken by the Roman Catholic Church and many Protestants
  - from the moment of fertilisation, a new person with potential, a human being complete with a soul, has come into existence
- At birth
  - the **pro-choice** view
  - independent life starts only at birth; until that point the foetus is totally dependent on the mother
- **Viability**
  - the view taken by the law
  - the foetus has rights from the point at which, if born, it could have a reasonable chance of survival (currently taken to be 24 weeks)
- A gradual process
  - the view of many Protestants
  - the embryo has the right to respect from conception, but full rights are acquired as the foetus develops (e.g. development of the nervous system, brain activity)

Alternatives to abortion

- the mother keeping the baby
- fostering until the mother can care for the baby herself
- adoption

'I chose you before I gave you life' (Jeremiah 1:5)

Pro-life
- (+) The baby's right to life is respected
- (+) The mother will not suffer the guilt feelings that are common after abortion
- (+) As well as support from the state, many church organisations will give her all the financial and emotional support she and her baby need
- (+) Infertile couples are given great joy and the child has a loving home

Pro-life
- (−) The mother and baby might struggle throughout life without access to support
- (−) The child might spend his/her whole childhood in foster care because the mother is not ready for the responsibility but does not want the child to be adopted and he/she may feel unwanted by the mother
- (−) There may be emotional problems later for all concerned when an adopted child wants to find his/her mother

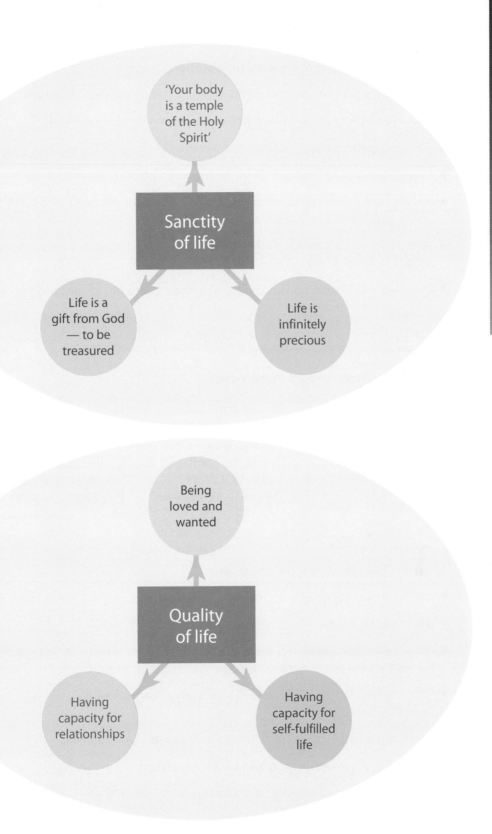

Roman Catholic Church views on abortion

- Abortion is a grave sin tantamount to murder, incurring **excommunication**.

- Human being with potential — the embryo has full rights from the start.

- Absolutely defenceless — merits special protection.

- Infinitely precious to God.

- All lives have potential and are of equal value — not for humans to pass judgement on the quality of life for a disabled foetus.

- Wrong to punish a child for his/her father's sin in case of rape — birth of child is good coming out of evil.

- The unwanted child can be adopted — brings joy to infertile couples and the chance of life and love for the child.

- Practical and emotional support given by Roman Catholic community and charities can enable young mothers to cope.

NB Some Protestants hold these views.

'Do not commit murder' (Exodus 20:13)

'Children are a gift from the Lord' (Psalm 127:3)

'…you must clothe yourself with compassion, kindness…' (Colossians 3:12)

Anglican Church views on abortion

- Abortion is a great moral evil — concern about the number of abortions taking place.

- Life is sacred and the foetus deserves respect and protection.

- But in certain circumstances, abortion may be the lesser of two evils — e.g. to save the mother's life and in cases of extreme distress, such as rape.

- Late abortions (i.e. after 24 weeks) for disability — only where the child would die soon after birth.

- Abortions up to 24 weeks for disability if in the child's best interests.

- Importance of compassion and love for all concerned.

- A matter for personal decision, in accordance with conscience.

Methodist Church views on abortion

- Similar to Anglican view — abortion is undesirable, but sometimes the lesser of two evils.

- Justified in some cases — risk to life/health of the mother and existing family, extreme poverty, rape, severe disability.

 Case study

Joanna Jepson

- Born in 1976
- An Anglican priest
- Had many years of operations to correct a jaw defect, for which she had suffered bullying at school
- Has a brother who has Down's Syndrome
- In 2001 she took the West Mercia police to court for not investigating the late abortion of a foetus with a cleft palate — she regarded this as unlawful killing
- Her complaint was dismissed

TopFoto

'When my bones were being formed…you knew that I was there — you saw me before I was born' (Psalm 139:15–16)

'Surely you know that you are God's temple and that God's Spirit lives in you' (1 Corinthians 3:16)

 Key words

abortion
autonomy
conception
embryo
excommunication
foetus
pro-choice
pro-life
secular
viability

'Then the Lord God formed a man… he breathed life-giving breath into his nostrils and the man began to live' (Genesis 2:7)

Test yourself

1 Fill in each of the gaps with what you think is the correct word in the following paragraphs:

Christians believe that human life is s............................. That means it is infinitely
p........................ and should be p............................. Many Christians also believe that
good q........................ of l............................. is important. Sometimes these two principles
conflict with each other.

Because of this, Roman Catholics think that those who have abortions are committing
a very serious s............................. They are therefore e............................. from the Church.
They think that a d............................. baby has the same right to life as anyone else and
that people should not pass judgement on its q............................. of life. They believe that,
if a woman who is pregnant as a result of r............................. goes through with the
pregnancy, then g............................. has triumphed over e............................. and the baby is
not being p............................. for what its father did.

Christians of other denominations also believe that human life is s.............................
and should be p............................. At the same time, they believe that sometimes abortion
is the l............................. of t............................. e............................. They think this especially if
the mother's l............................. is in d............................., if she has been r............................. or
if the baby is unlikely to l............................. for very long because of serious d.............................
In these cases, they believe that abortion may be the most c............................. and
l............................. action to take. They think that the d............................. is a personal one,
made in accordance with c.............................

2 What is meant by the term abortion?

3 What is meant by pro-life and pro-choice?

4 Explain two answers that are given to the question of when meaningful life begins.

Exam tip

Ensure that you understand Christian beliefs and teachings on every topic set for study. It may help you when you are revising to have a postcard for each topic. Note down four beliefs or teachings relating to each of the topics.

Examination question

'Any action to prevent the birth of an unwanted child is the most loving thing to do.'

Do you agree? Give reasons for your answer, showing that you have thought about more than one point of view. *(6 marks)*

Euthanasia

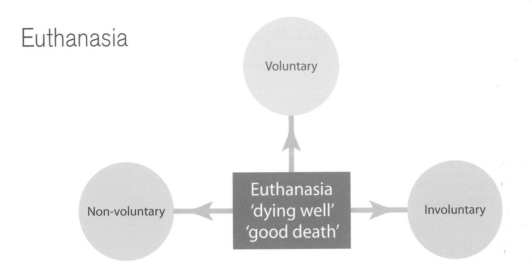

Euthanasia is often explained as 'mercy killing' or 'dying with dignity'.

Voluntary euthanasia refers to the request by a person for the doctor to end a life of intolerable suffering or loss of dignity.

Non-voluntary euthanasia refers to a situation where a person is incapable of making a request, e.g. is in a long-term coma or cannot communicate at all. Euthanasia is thought to be in that individual's best interests and what he/she would have wanted.

Involuntary euthanasia refers to the kind of practice that went on in Nazi Germany, where a person is put to death without being consulted and with no thought given to the best interests of that individual.

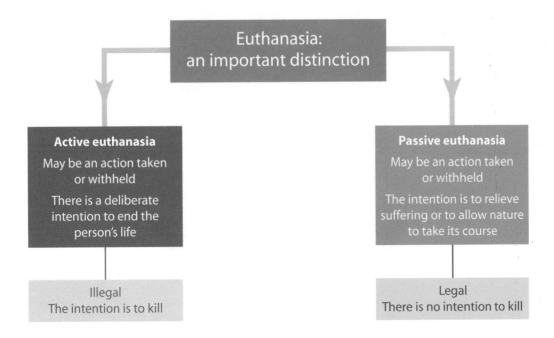

Active euthanasia: some difficult decisions

For	Against
The right to self-determination — it is genuinely what the patient wants	Can one be sure it is real and lasting desire? Might it be due to feelings of pressure?
No animal would be made to suffer continual intolerable pain, so why should a human being?	Improvements in palliative care make it unnecessary
Feeding tubes simply prolong the dying of PVS patients and are just a form of medical treatment	Feeding tubes are a form of basic care to which everyone has an absolute right

Passive euthanasia: some difficult decisions

For	Against
Giving a high dose of morphine may shorten life, but its intention is to relieve pain	Is relief of pain the only motive in giving morphine? If not, it just prolongs dying
Withholding or withdrawing treatment that has no useful purpose allows nature to take its course	Withholding or withdrawing treatment just prolongs the suffering and is cruel
The law protects the majority of society from harmful consequences of allowing euthanasia	Suicide is legal; not to allow disabled people help with dying from doctors is discrimination

Dignity in Dying

Campaigns to legalise:

- voluntary euthanasia
- **living wills**

The ProLife Alliance

Campaigns to promote:

- the right to life as fundamental
- the provision of more hospices

Diane Pretty claimed that not allowing her to commit assisted suicide was an act of discrimination

Case study

The hospice movement

- Founded by Cicely Saunders
- Place of rest for terminally and incurably ill
- Some are residential, some primarily or only day care
- Some are specialist units for children or teenagers, with accommodation for family
- Based on belief that all people have the right to be given the best possible care, be shown absolute respect and to die with dignity
- Provision of **palliative care** to enable quality of life right up to death
- Other forms of therapy often available
- Counselling for both patient and family as preparation for death

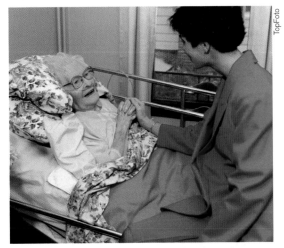

Hospices enable patients to die with dignity

'Everything that happens in this world happens at the time God chooses. He sets the time for birth and the time for death' (Ecclesiastes 3:1–2)

'Do not commit murder' (Exodus 20:13)

Views of most Christian Churches on euthanasia

- Totally opposed to all forms of active euthanasia.
- God gave life and only he has the right to take it: euthanasia is 'playing God'.
- The body is a 'temple of the Holy Spirit' and so is sacred (1 Corinthians 6:19).
- It breaks the commandment: do not commit murder.
- God's gift of the power of responsible decision-making, i.e. **self-determination**, has limits: it does not include taking one's own life, as that is not responsible **stewardship**.
- It shows a lack of trust in God's love, compassion and mercy.
- It makes judgements about someone's value and quality of life that are not for humans to make: in God's eyes all humans are of equal value, whatever their circumstances.
- It deprives vulnerable people of protection from abuse.
- It leads to a slippery slope that might permit first voluntary, then non-voluntary and maybe, ultimately, involuntary euthanasia.

Views of some individual Christians

- Life is sacred and should normally be preserved, but not at all costs.

- Quality of life is more important than biological existence — death is preferable to a miserable existence (as stated in Ecclesiastes).

- God would not want people to undergo intolerable suffering or complete loss of dignity — this is not what it means to be 'in God's image'.

- The decision for euthanasia may be an act of responsible decision-making and a way of enabling God's will for the individual to be done.

- Euthanasia may be the most compassionate option, especially in those cases where pain cannot be relieved and where the person is totally dependent for everything on others.

- Death is easier to come to terms with and face if the fear of intolerable suffering is removed.

NB Although the mainstream denominations are all opposed to it, many individuals within those churches support the legalising of voluntary euthanasia, and some individual church leaders support it.

 Case study

Lilian Boyes and Dr Nigel Cox

- Lilian Boyes suffered from rheumatoid arthritis
- Her consultant was Dr Nigel Cox
- In 1991 she was admitted to hospital
- She was always in extreme pain and could not bear anyone to touch her or hold her hand
- She repeatedly asked Dr Cox to give her a lethal injection
- Eventually out of compassion he gave her an injection of potassium chloride, which was not a painkiller but would stop her heart
- He entered this in the hospital notes and it was when these were later checked that he was reported for his action
- In 1992 he was convicted of attempted murder, but was given a suspended prison sentence
- He was allowed to continue practising medicine

Key words

active euthanasia

euthanasia

involuntary euthanasia

living wills

non-voluntary euthanasia

palliative care

passive euthanasia

self-determination

stewardship

the hospice movement

voluntary euthanasia

Test yourself

1 **True or false?**   TRUE FALSE

   Voluntary euthanasia is illegal but non-voluntary euthanasia is legal in the UK.

   Active euthanasia is illegal but passive euthanasia is legal in the UK.

Giving a cancer patient morphine to relieve pain, even though it will shorten the person's life, is allowed in UK law.

The Anglican Church agrees with voluntary euthanasia.

The Roman Catholic Church agrees with voluntary euthanasia.

Hospices are homes for the elderly.

Hospices specialise in palliative care.

There are hospices for children.

Dignity in Dying is an organisation that opposes legalising voluntary euthanasia.

The ProLife Alliance opposes legalising voluntary euthanasia.

2 Explain how belief in the sanctity of life might influence a Christian's attitude to voluntary euthanasia.

> 'So God created human beings, making them to be like himself' (Genesis 1:27)

> 'Help to carry one another's burdens, and in this way you will obey the law of Christ' (Galatians 6:2)

> 'Happy are those who are merciful to others; God will be merciful to them' (Matthew 5:7)

Examination question

'When people are suffering unbearable pain, voluntary euthanasia is the kindest action to take.'

Do you agree? Give reasons for your answer, showing that you have thought about more than one point of view. Refer to Christian arguments in your answer. *(6 marks)*

Exam tip

When answering a 6-mark evaluation question, remember that to reach more than level 3 you need to include relevant reference to Christian arguments. This may consist of reference to biblical texts, Church teachings or general Christian principles.

The use of medical technology

Fertility treatments

Infertility is caused by a variety of factors. Sometimes the problem can be solved, but often couples have to resort to particular types of **fertility treatment**. The distress caused by infertility has been compared to that caused by bereavement: it is intense and long lasting, if not permanent. It creates a sense of inadequacy, failure and emptiness. The Old Testament story of Hannah (1 Samuel 1) illustrates the effects.

> 'Help to carry one another's burdens, and in this way you will obey the law of Christ' (Galatians 6:2)

> Her husband…would ask her: 'Hannah, why are you crying? Why won't you eat? Why are you always so sad? Don't I mean more to you than ten sons?' (1 Samuel 1:8)

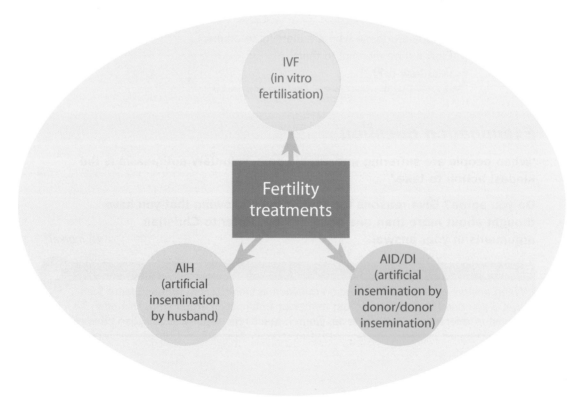

IVF
(in vitro fertilisation)

Fertility treatments

AIH
(artificial insemination by husband)

AID/DI
(artificial insemination by donor/donor insemination)

Methods of treatment

- **AIH:**
  - the husband's/partner's sperm is collected and inserted into the woman's vagina; fertilisation is left to occur naturally
- **AID/DI:**
  - as for AIH, but with the use of donors who have been paid a small sum to donate sperm to a donor bank; the husband's name appears on the birth certificate, but at 18 children have the right to know the identity of their genetic fathers
- **IVF:**
  - hormonal treatment increases the number of eggs that ripen; at maturity they are collected and put in a dish, to be fertilised with the sperm that has been collected; after checks for viability one or two embryos are put into the uterus
  - spare embryos may be frozen for up to ten years; they may be used for future cycles of treatment, donated to other infertile couples or donated for **embryonic research**; otherwise they are destroyed
  - both partners must agree about the use of any spare embryos

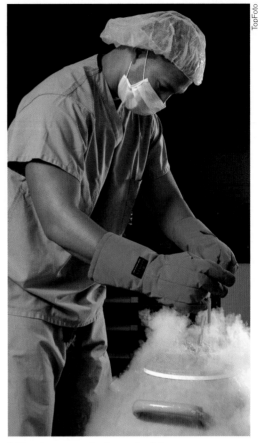

IVF embryos may be frozen for future use

Embryonic research

This is regulated by the **HFEA** (Human Fertilisation and Embryology Authority), which gives licences to research institutions for specific purposes. It is to be used only when there is no alternative and was originally permitted only for the study of infertility and miscarriage, though it has now been extended (see the section on cloning on pages 29–32).

The embryo must be destroyed at 14 days, as that is when the primitive streak (the beginning of what will eventually be the nervous system) appears. After 14 days there is no further possibility of the embryo dividing to form twins or recombining, and so it could be said that from that point the embryo is in some sense an individual.

> 'So God created human beings, making them to be like himself. He created them male and female, blessed them, and said, "Have many children..."'
> (Genesis 1:27–28)

> 'When my bones were being formed...you knew that I was there — you saw me before I was born'
> (Psalm 139:15–16)

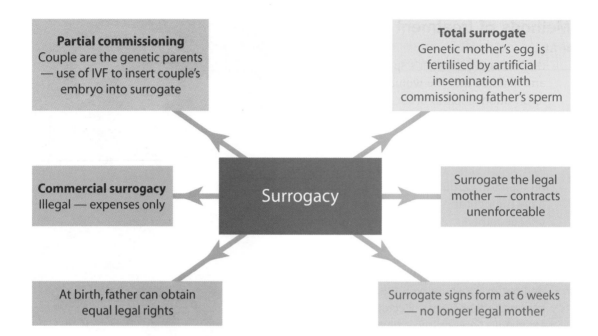

Abraham and Hagar

- Some people claim that the story recorded in Genesis 16 is an early example of surrogacy.
- Because of his wife's infertility, Abraham had a child by her slave and this child was then to be classed as Sarah's.
- This was a very ancient custom and is not a parallel to modern surrogacy — Abraham had a sexual relationship with Hagar to enable her to conceive.

Roman Catholic views on fertility treatment and surrogacy

- A child is a gift from God, not a right or a commodity to be ordered. Infertility is distressing, but there is the possibility of adoption or fostering.

- All forms of fertility treatment interfere with nature by separating the **unitive** from the **procreative** aspect of the sexual relationship and they also involve masturbation, which is seen as unnatural and therefore sinful.

- The use of donated sperm is described as a form of 'mechanical adultery' since it brings a third party into the relationship and it may cause social and psychological problems later.

- The creation of spare embryos with the possibility of their being researched on and then destroyed disregards the **sanctity of life** and is tantamount to murder. It exploits the most defenceless of God's creatures: embryos of less than 14 days, which makes IVF particularly sinful.

- **Surrogacy** is seen as reducing the mysterious and wonderful process of conception to what has been called a barnyard procedure.

Protestant views on fertility treatment and surrogacy

- Most Protestants see most forms as a responsible use by doctors of the skills given to them by God.

- It is an act of compassion, fulfilling the command to 'love your neighbour', as infertility is a source of great and lasting distress to couples. Children are a blessing and enrich a marriage and are what God intended at creation.

- It is not interfering with nature, but is putting faulty nature right.

- Many Protestants share the same concerns as Roman Catholics about the possibility of social and psychological problems arising from the use of donated sperm, however, and are opposed to AID and IVF that uses donor sperm.

- Some, however, see sperm donation as simply another form of fertilisation and, as long as donors are not paid, as an act of love.

- Many accept the use of spare embryos for research as they are not used after 14 days and the research is only for very serious reasons. At that early stage the embryo is a potential human being whose rights develop with greater maturity so, although it should be treated with respect, it does not have the absolute right to life.

- Some take the same view on embryonic research as that of the Roman Catholic Church.

- Most Christians oppose surrogacy more out of concern for its possible commercialisation of human life and for the social and psychological problems that might arise. The Anglican Church has stated its opposition to it.

- Some accept surrogacy in certain situations as an act of self-sacrificial love and compassion on the part of the surrogate.

'Everything that happens in this world happens at the time God chooses.
He sets the time for birth and the time for death'
(Ecclesiastes 3:1–2)

'Children are a gift from the Lord; they are a real blessing'
(Psalm 127:3)

Key words
AID/DI
AIH
embryonic research
fertility treatment
HFEA
infertility
IVF
procreative
sanctity of life
surrogacy
unitive

Test yourself

Case study

Kim Cotton and COTS

Surrogate mother Kim Cotton

- She was the UK's first commercial surrogate mother and was paid £6,500
- She then sold her story to a newspaper for a huge sum
- She provided the egg, which was inseminated with the commissioning father's sperm
- She has never had any contact with the child or the parents and still finds this hard
- She later carried a child (without a fee) for an infertile friend and the relationship is still close
- She founded COTS (Childlessness Overcome through Surrogacy) as a non-profit-making introduction agency for surrogates and infertile couples
- She left COTS (though is still a patron) because of a series of scandals, e.g. huge sums of money being paid to surrogates; surrogates refusing to hand the child over or having abortions; commissioning parents not wanting the child after it was born
- She is still convinced of the value of surrogacy and claims that most work out well for the surrogates, the parents and the children
- She prefers partial (host surrogacy), because that creates fewer emotional problems for the surrogate

1 Give three arguments in favour of surrogacy.

2 Give three arguments against surrogacy.

3 Explain why some Christians disagree with the use of IVF.

4 Explain why some Christians accept the use of IVF.

> '...you must clothe yourself with compassion, kindness...' (Colossians 3:12)

Examination question

'Becoming a surrogate mother is an act of Christian compassion.'

What do you think? Explain your opinion. *(3 marks)*

Exam tip

3-mark evaluation questions do not require you to give two points of view. They want you to say what you think about the issue, giving reasons for the opinion you hold. You need to make sure that you read the stem (the quotation at the start of the question) very carefully so that your answer is focused and relevant.

Genetic engineering

Genetic engineering refers to changes made to the genetic structure of living things. Human genetic engineering is permitted for two types of **gene therapy**: **somatic cell therapy** and the creation of **saviour siblings**. Some people would like to take genetic engineering further and create **designer babies**.

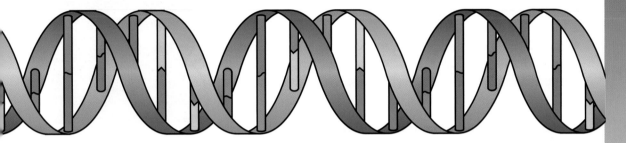

Somatic cell therapy

This is a treatment that adds to, enhances or replaces a defective gene. It is a treatment for single genetic disorders such as X-SCID (X-linked severe combined immunodeficiency), which means that any infection is likely to prove fatal.

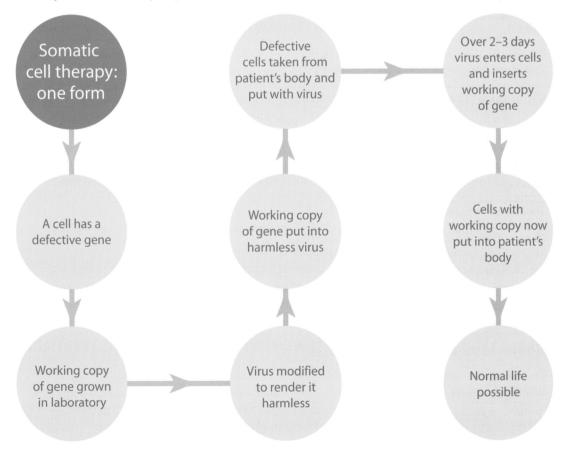

Case study

Rhys Evans

- Failure to respond to antibiotic treatment for infection
- Admitted to hospital
- Daily uncertainty about his survival
- Diagnosed with X-SCID
- In 2002 became first child in UK to receive somatic cell therapy
- Now a healthy schoolboy

TopFoto

Christian attitudes to somatic cell therapy

For	Against
Mainstream churches, including the Roman Catholic Church, regard it as morally acceptable, since it is aimed at healing the individual	Some individual Christians oppose it although they accept its intentions are good
It saves life	It may be only short-term saving of life
It is an extension of Jesus' healing ministry that is now the responsibility of his followers	Jesus did not heal everyone who was sick, and there are limits to this also today
It is an act of compassion	Is it compassionate to give a treatment whose long-term success is not known?
Development and refinement of the technique is a responsible use of God-given skills	Concern that those developing the techniques might have mixed motives — wanting to be the first to develop something new and be famous
The benefits outweigh the risks	Very risky — one French child developed leukaemia as a result of somatic cell therapy
How can a price be put on the life of a child?	Should large sums of money be spent on very rare conditions when more common conditions need treatments and when thousands are dying of hunger etc. in poor countries?
It is less expensive than current treatments, so shows good stewardship of limited resources	As above
Strictly regulated by the HFEA	Concerns of a slippery slope leading to legalisation of germline therapy (where future generations will be affected), and designer babies

Saviour siblings

This technique is used to save the life of children who have a life-threatening disorder. In the UK, every treatment has to be approved by the HFEA. The treatment combines IVF with PGD (**pre-implantation genetic diagnosis**), which is a form of genetic screening. If a baby free from the disorder is born, its cord blood can be used to treat the sick sibling.

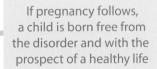

| Saviour siblings: the process | → | IVF is used to produce embryos that are then screened for signs of the disorder | → | Embryos free from the disorder and a close match with the sick child are selected for insertion into the woman |

| Stem cells from the baby's cord blood are transplanted into the sick sibling | ← | If pregnancy follows, a child is born free from the disorder and with the prospect of a healthy life | ← |

 Case study

Adam and Molly Nash

The Nash family

- Molly Nash was born with a genetic disorder that would lead to an early death
- Her parents wanted another child — but one free from the disorder
- They also wanted treatment for Molly
- Through a combination of IVF and PGD Mrs Nash conceived and gave birth to Adam, a healthy baby free from the disorder
- The stem cells from his cord blood were used to give Molly a bone marrow transplant, which was a success

Christian attitudes to saviour siblings

For	Against
Some Protestant churches accept it, provided the saviour sibling is genuinely wanted for him/herself	Roman Catholic Church and some Protestant Christians oppose it
It is saving life, which is a good thing, so fulfils the sanctity of life principle	The destruction of embryos that are not selected breaches the sanctity of life principle
It promotes quality of life for both children	Quality of life concerns should not override sanctity of life
It is an act of compassion	
PGD is a responsible use of God-given skills where there is a high risk of a serious genetic disorder	Screening for and destroying 'defective' embryos is similar to what Hitler did in his compulsory euthanasia policies and in the holocaust
IVF is an acceptable procedure and also a responsible use of God-given skills	The use of IVF is morally unacceptable for the reasons given in the previous section
If the baby is genuinely wanted for him/herself there is no exploitation — only cord blood (which would be discarded) is being used	It is a form of exploitation — the saviour sibling's interests and possible wishes do not come first
The bond between the siblings will be intensified and the saviour sibling will feel very special as he/she learns about what has happened	There could be serious psychological and social problems for the saviour sibling should the treatment fail

Designer babies

What is lawful in the UK:

- Saviour siblings are a kind of designer baby, since their genetic make-up is selected to be as close as possible to that of the sick sibling.
- The use of sex selection where there is a sex-linked genetic disorder.

What is not lawful in the UK:

- Sex selection for social reasons.
- Research into ways of enabling couples to choose the appearance, intellectual or sporting potential of children.

'Do not commit murder'
(Exodus 20:13)

Jesus called the twelve disciples...
Then he sent them out...to heal the sick'
(Luke 9:1–2)

Christian attitudes to designer babies

■ For the different views on saviour siblings, see the table above

■ Roman Catholics and some Protestant Christians object to sex selection as a form of gene therapy
  - It involves the use of IVF, which is unacceptable to Roman Catholics.
  - It involves the destruction of embryos, which breaches the sanctity of life principle and the right of every individual to be treated as a person from conception.
  - It could encourage gender discrimination.
  - It could have serious social consequences as a result of gender imbalance.

■ Many Protestant Christians accept sex selection for therapeutic reasons
  - It enables parents to have a child free from serious genetic disorders.
  - It is a responsible use of God-given skills.
  - It is an act of compassion.
  - It supports the quality of life principle.

■ All the mainstream churches are opposed to non-therapeutic genetic engineering (i.e. creating designer babies for appearance etc.)
  - It encourages a form of **idolatry**, e.g. the worship of beauty.
  - It makes a child a commodity (like ordering designer clothes) rather than a gift.
  - It places a terrible burden on the child to live up to expectations.
  - If it is unsuccessful, the consequences for the child could be disastrous.
  - It might lead to a two-tier society and discrimination, based on who could afford the treatment.

■ Some Christians might support non-therapeutic genetic engineering
  - In rare cases, sex selection for social reasons could be an act of compassion for parents (see the Case study below).
  - It is natural for parents to want the best for their children, so they should be able to choose what would lead to their children being successful and so on.

> **Key words**
>
> designer babies
> gene therapy
> genetic engineering
> idolatry
> pre-implantation genetic diagnosis
> saviour siblings
> somatic cell therapy

Test yourself

Case study

The Masterson family

■ Mr and Mrs Masterson wanted permission to have IVF and PGD in order to select the sex of their next child
■ They already had four young sons

- Their only daughter had been killed in an accident
- They wanted another child, but did not want another boy
- Permission was refused because the selection was for social reasons
- Sex selection is permitted only when it is to prevent serious genetic conditions from being passed on

1 Give two reasons why some Christians might agree with sex selection in the Mastersons' case.

2 Give two reasons why some Christians might disagree with it.

3 Why might many Christians agree with the development and use of somatic cell therapy?

4 Why might some Christians oppose it?

Examination question

a What is meant by the term saviour sibling? *(2 marks)*

b 'Christian parents with a very sick child should never agree to the creation of a saviour sibling.'

Do you agree? Give reasons for your answer, showing that you have thought about more than one point of view. *(6 marks)*

Exam tip

To gain more than 4 marks in a 6-mark evaluation question, you have to argue from more than one viewpoint.

Cloning

Cloning consists of creating a genetically identical copy of an organism. As a result of the successful cloning of Dolly the sheep, the attention of some medical scientists turned to humans.

Reproductive cloning

Reproductive cloning is aimed at creating human life.

> 'Worship no god but me.
> Do not make for yourselves images'
> (Exodus 20:3–4)

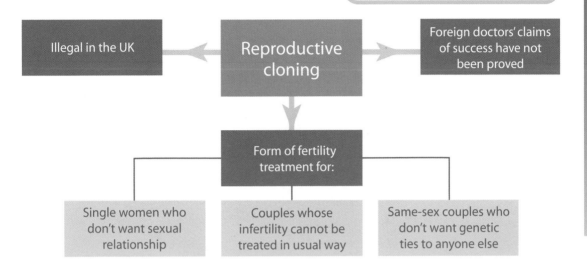

Illegal in the UK	**Reproductive cloning**	Foreign doctors' claims of success have not been proved

Form of fertility treatment for:

Single women who don't want sexual relationship	Couples whose infertility cannot be treated in usual way	Same-sex couples who don't want genetic ties to anyone else

Christian views on reproductive cloning

- All Christian churches and most individual Christians view it as morally wrong.

- 'Playing God' with potential for disastrous social and psychological consequences.

- Idolatrous to want a copy of oneself.

- Unnatural, especially when used by same-sex or single people.

- It shows disrespect for the dignity of humanity by separating conception from the mutual self-giving act of sexual intercourse and from sexuality itself.

- Exploitation of the embryo.

- The child is a manufactured product, a commodity not a gift.

- Creates biological confusion.

- Scientists pushing for it motivated by desire for fame.

- Creation of Dolly the sheep was preceded by hundreds of failed attempts (stillbirths, deformed foetuses etc.) and she died prematurely; unlikely to be different with human cloning.

- Danger of reducing the gene pool.

- A few Christians might see it as an act of compassion towards those for whom other forms of fertility treatment are not suitable.

- Scientific progress may assist evolution of better form of human species.

Therapeutic cloning

Therapeutic cloning is aimed at researching ways into curing a wide variety of diseases (e.g. motor neurone, Alzheimer's) and conditions (e.g. spinal injuries). It may be carried out only in institutes licensed by the HFEA to do so and the embryos must be destroyed at 14 days. It studies how:

- **embryonic stem cells** (which are pluripotent) become specialised cells
- cells become diseased

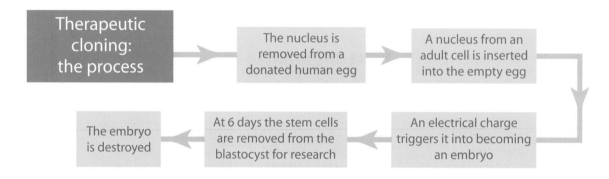

Roman Catholic views on therapeutic cloning

- Morally unacceptable.

- Destruction of the embryo shows disrespect and is tantamount to murder.

- A form of 'biological slavery' ('The Dignity of a Person').

- Human life is being treated as disposable biological material.

- Exploitation.

- The use of adult stem cells provides a viable alternative.

NB Many Christians from other denominations are also opposed to therapeutic cloning for all or some of the reasons given above.

Protestant views on therapeutic cloning

- Act of compassion for those suffering from terrible physical conditions.

- Acceptable use of God-given intelligence and skills.

- Extension of Christ's healing work.

- Before 14 days the embryo is not human life in any meaningful sense, i.e. a person.

- Acceptable as there is no valid alternative — **adult stem cells** more limited in usefulness.

The use of hybrid embryos

For one successful harvesting of stem cells from a cloned embryo, hundreds of attempts have to be made. There is a serious shortage of donated human eggs and so, in 2008, Parliament voted to allow the use of **hybrid embryos** in research. Hybrid embryos are created through inserting human genetic material into empty eggs from cows. Again, licences for this have to be obtained and the embryos must be destroyed.

Christian views on use of hybrid embryos

- Roman Catholics are totally opposed
  - seen as blasphemous and as 'playing God'
  - total opposition to any form of therapeutic cloning (see above)

- Many Protestant Christians are very uneasy
  - concerns that boundaries will continue to be pushed back
  - possible slippery slope to treating embryos simply as research material

- Some Protestant Christians see it as having great potential for speeding up research and development of treatments.

 Case study

Christopher Reeve (1952–2004)

- A very gifted man
  - actor
  - sportsman
  - pianist
  - author
  - public speaker
- His most famous acting role was in the *Superman* films
- Political activist
  - environmental issues
  - protested against the Vietnam War
  - protested against Pinochet's death warrants against actors in Chile
  - involved with Amnesty International and Save the Children
- Falling from a horse caused severe spinal cord injuries
- Totally dependent on others for washing, moving etc.
- On ventilator until he received a new treatment in 2003
- Worked to raise awareness in USA about spinal cord injuries
- Lobbied for ending ban on funding embryonic stem cell research in USA
  - believed it would lead to successful treatment for injuries like his
  - made it a high profile campaign

TopFoto

The *Superman* films were highly successful

Key words

adult stem cells

cloning

embryonic stem cells

hybrid embryos

reproductive cloning

therapeutic cloning

Test yourself

I can't understand why people are against embryonic stem cell cloning. It could lead to cures for so many illnesses and to being able to repair organ damage. It could help paralysed people walk again, just like Jesus cured a paralysed man. So many people could have a better quality of life.

But it's not just about quality of life. What about sanctity of life? In stem cell research, embryos are created and then killed. What respect for human life does that show? And eventually someone will use the same technology to create human clones. Just because scientists can do something, it doesn't mean they should — there are limits to what they should do.

1 Explain the different purposes of reproductive and therapeutic cloning.

2 Explain why some Christians are against therapeutic cloning.

3 Explain why some Christians support therapeutic cloning.

4 Why do many Christians who support therapeutic cloning disagree with the creation of hybrid embryos for that research?

Examination question

Explain why most Christians oppose reproductive cloning.　　　*(3 marks)*

Exam tip

Before answering a question, always think about the command (trigger) word. This is the word, usually at the start of a question, that tells you what you have to do. The command (trigger) word 'explain' requires you to show both knowledge and understanding. You need to develop the points you make, rather than give a simple list of points.

Sexual relationships

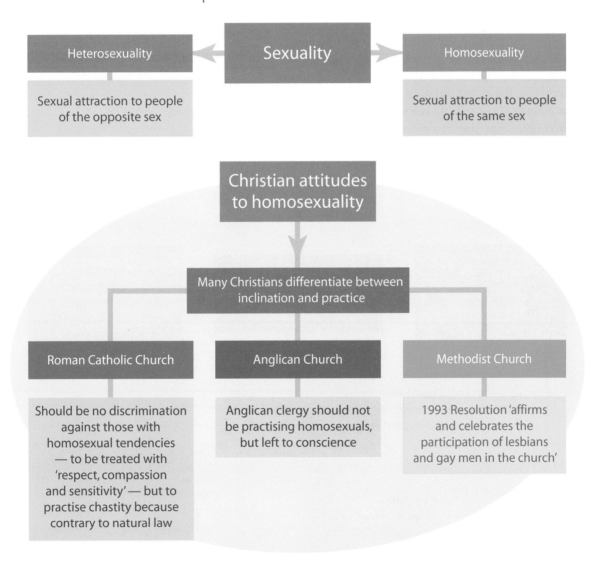

Heterosexuality	←	Sexuality	→	Homosexuality

Sexual attraction to people of the opposite sex

Sexual attraction to people of the same sex

Christian attitudes to homosexuality

Many Christians differentiate between inclination and practice

Roman Catholic Church	Anglican Church	Methodist Church
Should be no discrimination against those with homosexual tendencies — to be treated with 'respect, compassion and sensitivity' — but to practise chastity because contrary to natural law	Anglican clergy should not be practising homosexuals, but left to conscience	1993 Resolution 'affirms and celebrates the participation of lesbians and gay men in the church'

Some Christians believe that the Bible's teachings were inspired by God and so are inerrant: they must always be obeyed. Same-sex relationships are therefore against God's will	← **'No man is to have sexual relations with another man'** **(Leviticus 18:22)** Both Old and New Testament teachings take the same attitude →	Some Christians believe that the Bible's teachings are to be respected, but they are not inerrant. Their writers were influenced by the culture of the day which did not embrace the loving same-sex partnerships seen today

Heterosexual relationships

The age of consent for sexual intercourse is 16 years, to prevent the exploitation of and harm to young people. Nevertheless, many teenagers have sexual relationships before that age. Attitudes to sex outside marriage have changed for a number of reasons:

- availability of reliable **contraception**
- couples marrying at a much later age than in previous decades
- decrease in influence of religious teachings
- promotion of sexual relationships at an early age by the media

> 'So God created human beings, making them to be like himself. He created them male and female, blessed them, and said, "Have many children…"' (Genesis 1:27–28)

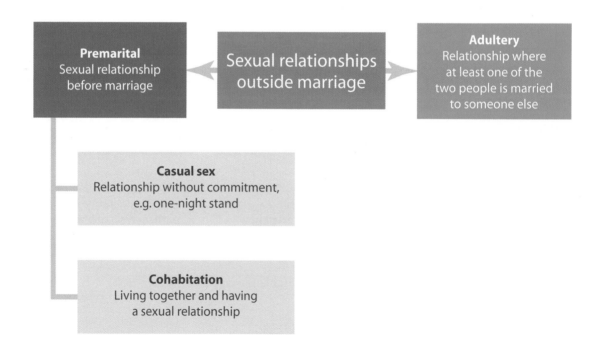

Premarital
Sexual relationship before marriage

← **Sexual relationships outside marriage** →

Adultery
Relationship where at least one of the two people is married to someone else

Casual sex
Relationship without commitment, e.g. one-night stand

Cohabitation
Living together and having a sexual relationship

Church teachings about heterosexual relationships

- **Sexuality** is a precious gift from God
  - it is an integral part of being human
  - it should be celebrated and enjoyed responsibly
  - self-control is essential for its joys to be most fully experienced
  - it involves and affects the whole person
  - casual sex shows disrespect and a lack of responsibility towards oneself and the other person; it trivialises sex
  - sexual relationships are best within marriage
  - marriage provides the level of commitment, trust etc. needed for the fullest enjoyment of a relationship
  - gives stable environment for rearing children (for Roman Catholics, this is the primary purpose of sex)

- Encouragement of **chastity** before marriage

- **Adultery** is wrong
  - against the Ten Commandments and other biblical teachings
  - breaks marriage vows
  - causes deep hurt and sense of betrayal
  - loss of trust within relationship

Attitudes of some Christians to premarital sexual relationships

- Social changes, e.g. delay in age of marriage, make it unrealistic to wait until marriage for sexual relationship.

- Availability of reliable contraception means that sexual relationships can be enjoyed responsibly before marriage.

- Premarital relationship acceptable provided it is within the context of love and commitment.

 Case study

The Silver Ring Thing

- Began in 1996 in USA in response to high rate of teenage pregnancies
- Came to the UK in 2004
- Aims to give teenagers full access to facts about premarital sexual relationships
- Promotes chastity before marriage as
  - God's will for human beings
  - the best way of avoiding harmful physical and emotional effects of premarital sex

- 4-week course, after which those who commit to sexual abstinence before marriage may choose to wear a purity ring
- Lydia Playfoot accused her school of breaching her human rights when it forbade her to wear her purity ring but her appeal was rejected in 2007
- The judgement was that a purity ring was not an essential symbol of the Christian faith

Lydia Playfoot took her school to the High Court after she was banned from wearing her purity ring to school

Contraception

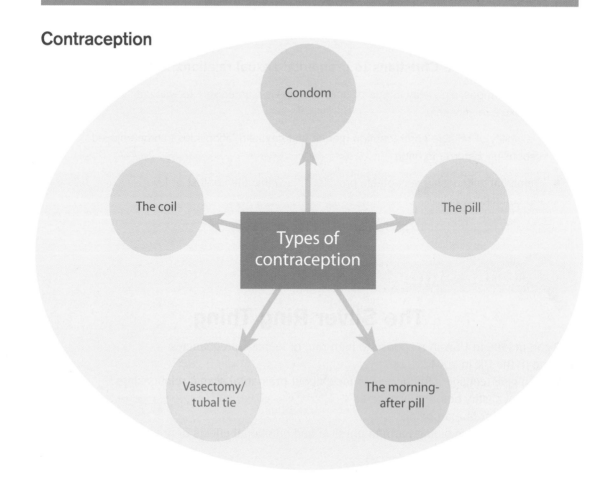

Roman Catholic teaching on contraception

- Contraception is sinful.

- The main purpose of sexual intercourse is procreative.

- Contraception either prevents pregnancy or acts as an abortifacient, which is tantamount to murder.

- Natural methods of family planning, e.g. tracking the rhythm of the menstrual cycle, are permitted as these do not set out to interfere with God's plan.

Protestant teaching on contraception

- It is acceptable.

- God gave humans the capacity for responsible decision-making and this includes decisions about having children.

- Procreation is not the primary purpose of sexual intercourse.

- There might be good reasons for not wanting children: poverty, wanting to space the births, a genetic disorder or the HIV virus carried by one partner.

- If unmarried people are determined to have sexual relationships, then using contraception is the responsible action to take.

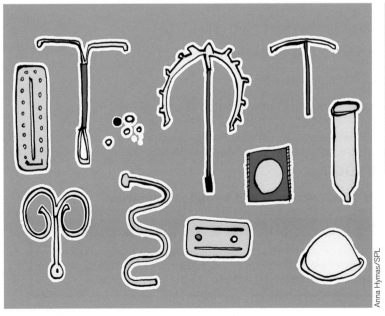

Anna Hymas/SPL

Key words

adultery

chastity

contraception

heterosexuality

homosexuality

premarital sexual relationships

sexuality

> 'God wants you to be holy and completely free from sexual immorality' (1 Thessalonians 4:3)

> 'Do not commit adultery' (Exodus 20:13)

> 'Children are a gift from the Lord; They are a real blessing' (Psalm 127:3)

> 'Avoid immorality…Don't you know that your body is the temple of the Holy Spirit…You do not belong to yourselves but to God; he bought you for a price. So use your bodies for God's glory' (1 Corinthians 6:18–20)

Test yourself

1 True or false?

TRUE FALSE

A sexual relationship between two people of the same sex is heterosexual.

A sexual relationship between two people before marriage is known as adultery.

The age of consent for sexual intercourse is 16 years.

Cohabitation is when two people live together.

The organisation that promotes chastity before marriage is the Golden Ring Thing.

Roman Catholics believe that the use of artificial contraception is sinful.

Roman Catholics believe that natural family planning methods are sinful.

Protestants believe that the main purpose of a sexual relationship is procreative.

All Christian churches teach that casual sex trivialises sex.

'Do not commit adultery' is one of the Ten Commandments.

2 Outline Church teachings about homosexuality.

3 Explain why Christians disagree about the interpretation of biblical teachings on homosexuality.

Examination question

Explain Christian beliefs about sexuality and sexual relationships. *(6 marks)*

Exam tip

There are no set biblical texts to learn in this unit. Nevertheless, being able to quote, paraphrase or refer to a few relevant texts or stories will help you to fill out and develop answers about Christian beliefs, teachings and attitudes to the set moral issues.

Drugs

A **drug** is a natural or artificial substance that has physical and/or emotional and mental effects when taken. These effects may be beneficial or harmful. Drugs may be legal, legal when prescribed by a doctor, or illegal.

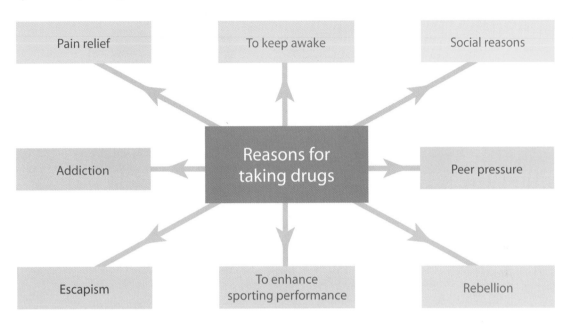

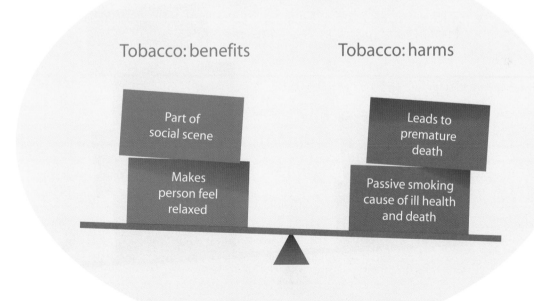

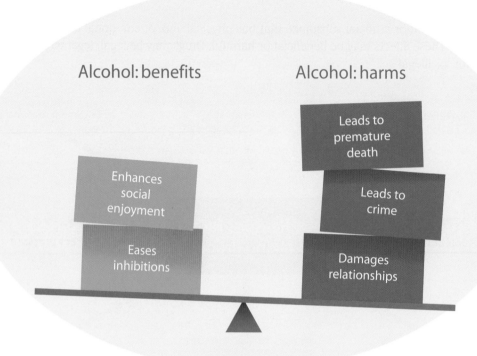

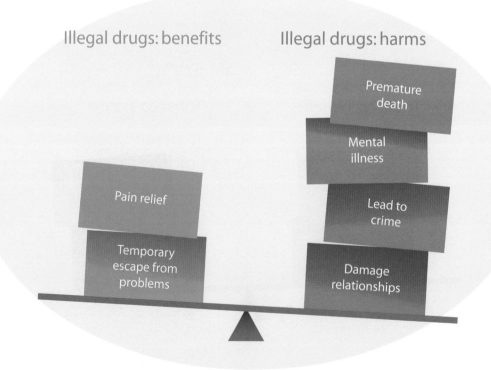

Christian attitudes to tobacco use

- Most discourage it because of the harm it causes to the smoker and those around.
- Seen as disrespect of body given by God and denial of sanctity of life.
- Not wise stewardship of money.

Attitude of Salvation Army to alcohol

- **Teetotal**.
- Don't want to set bad example to others.
- Disrespect to body given by God and denial of sanctity of life.
- Concerned about suffering caused to family of drinker by heavy drinking or **addiction**.
- Concerned about social problems.
- Gives practical help to those with drink problems and their families.

Attitude of many Christians to alcohol

- Drinking in moderation permissible
  - Jesus changed water into wine at a wedding and he drank wine himself
  - Psalm 104 refers to the joy that wine brings to life
  - but Proverbs warns that it makes people loud and foolish
- Shows disrespect to body only if taken in excess.
- Same concerns as Salvation Army relating to heavy drinking and addiction.
- Gives practical support to those with alcohol problems and their families.

Attitude of Christians to illegal drugs

- Goes against principles of both sanctity and quality of life.
- Opposed because of harm caused to individuals, families and society.
- Described by Pope John Paul XXIII as the new slavery — addiction removes freedom.
- Some Christians would agree to use of **cannabis** in treatment of certain serious medical conditions, e.g. multiple sclerosis.
- Some Christians support legalisation of cannabis — claim it is less dangerous than alcohol.
- Some are involved in treatment and **rehabilitation** of drug addicts.
- Drug addicts should be helped rather than denounced.
- The same as Jesus, who said he had come for those who needed him (Mark 2:17).

Yeldall Bridges

- A Christian centre providing residential rehabilitation for men aged 18–50 with serious drug or alcohol problems
- The initial programme lasts 3–6 months and includes:
  - individual and group therapy
  - learning about life skills, attitudes etc.
  - recreation, e.g. sport
  - daily work in the house or grounds
  - further skills training, e.g. literacy and numeracy, food hygiene
- The second stage lasts 3–4 months
- Residents live in flats and prepare for independent living
- After completing the programme, there is aftercare for up to a year

'Help to carry one another's burdens, and in this way you will obey the law of Christ' (Galatians 6:2)

'Aren't five sparrows sold for two pennies? Yet not one sparrow is forgotten by God. Even the hairs of your head have all been counted…you are worth much more than many sparrows' (Luke 12:6–7)

'Jesus called the twelve disciples…
Then he sent them out …to heal the sick' (Luke 9:1–2)

'Do not get drunk with wine…instead, be filled with the Spirit' (Ephesians 5:18)

'You created every part of me; you put me together in my mother's womb.' (Psalm 139:13)

'Surely you know that you are God's temple and that God's Spirit lives in you!' (1 Corinthians 3:16)

'What are human beings that you are mindful of them, mortals that you care for them?
Yet you have made them a little lower than God, and crowned them with glory and honour' (Psalm 8:4–5)

Key words	
addiction	rehabilitation
cannabis	teetotal
drug	

Test yourself

Case study

Jackie Pullinger

- She wanted to become a missionary and, in 1966, aged 22, she went to Hong Kong
- She became a primary teacher in the Walled City, the most deprived and dangerous part of Kowloon
- She opened a small youth club
- Many who came were members of Triad gangs and drug addicts
- Some became Christian and overcame their addiction
- She gave up her teaching job to concentrate on working with young people
- She opened a home for those who needed help
- She won the respect of one Triad leader, who promised not to hound any of the members of his gang who left through becoming Christian
- She and two missionaries have set up St Stephen's Society, a drug rehabilitation programme in Hong Kong and South East Asia

1 Explain how Jackie Pullinger's beliefs led her to work with drug addicts and Triad members in Hong Kong. Include references to Christian teachings in your answer.

2 Complete the four boxes in the diagram below by giving four effects of alcohol misuse

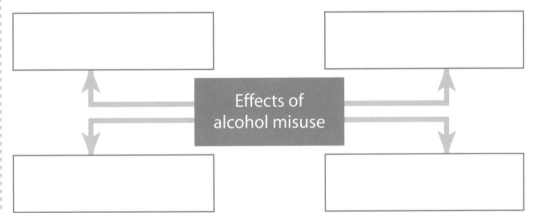

Effects of alcohol misuse

Examination question

Explain why Christians hold different views on drinking alcohol. *(6 marks)*

Exam tip

When you are asked to give different views, make sure that you do include more than one set of views otherwise you may lose half the available marks.

Social responsibility

Marriage

A **civil ceremony** may take place in a register office or in any place that has a licence to conduct weddings, e.g. a hotel or castle. These ceremonies are entirely secular. **Religious ceremonies** are held in a place of worship.

Because marriage is a legal contract that gives each partner rights, whether it is civil or religious in nature, it must be conducted by a legally authorised person for it to be valid.

Christian beliefs and teachings about marriage

- Most see it as a **sacramental covenant**, i.e. a sacred bond between the couple that has been made by God with the couple. The ring is a visible sign of this.

- It is intended to be for life, so solemn **vows** are made with God as witness, in which the couple promise to love and care for one another for the rest of their lives, whatever their circumstances may be, and to be faithful to one another.

A sign of lifelong love and faithfulness — marriage is permanent and exclusive

- It was part of God's plan right from the start; the creation story in Genesis 2 makes that clear.

- It enables the couple to experience the joy of sexual fulfilment and commitment.

- It provides a stable environment for rearing children.

- It enriches and strengthens society.

- It is a partnership of equals
  - Most Christians see this as meaning that roles are shared and decisions are joint.
  - A minority of Christians believe that husbands and wives have different roles and that wives are to obey their husbands.
  - The Roman Catholic Church teaches that every act of sexual intercourse should be open to the possibility of children as God's gift.

Alternatives to marriage

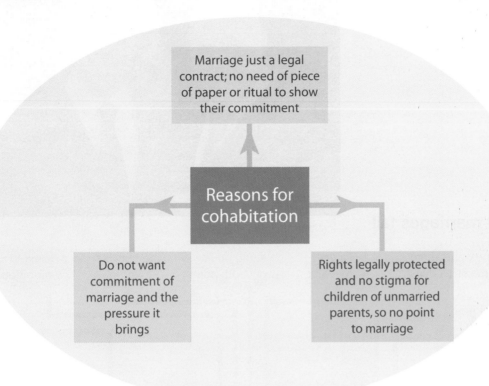

Marriage just a legal contract; no need of piece of paper or ritual to show their commitment

Reasons for cohabitation

Do not want commitment of marriage and the pressure it brings

Rights legally protected and no stigma for children of unmarried parents, so no point to marriage

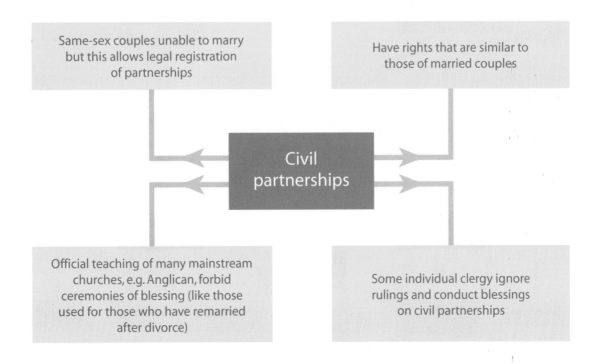

Same-sex couples unable to marry but this allows legal registration of partnerships

Have rights that are similar to those of married couples

Civil partnerships

Official teaching of many mainstream churches, e.g. Anglican, forbid ceremonies of blessing (like those used for those who have remarried after divorce)

Some individual clergy ignore rulings and conduct blessings on civil partnerships

Matt Lucas and Kevin McGee. Registering a civil partnership allows gay couples to enjoy the same rights as married couples

Reuters

Why marriages fail

One wants them and the other doesn't

Career comes first

Long hours away from home

Wife earns more

Husband not ambitious

Children from previous relationships

Loss of trust

Difficult children

Hurt

Children

Work

Infidelity

Sense of betrayal

Infertility

Long-term sickness

Debt

Disability

Changed circumstances

Why marriages fail

Money

Job loss

Married too young

Gambling

Immaturity

Addiction

Unreasonable behaviour

Boredom

False expectations

Constant nagging

Physical/mental cruelty

Drugs

Alcohol

Support for failing marriages

- the Roman Catholic Church has specific support agencies, e.g. Marriage Care, Accord
- marriage counsellors
- advice from a priest/minister
- reading the Bible
- prayer
- receiving the sacraments
- family and friends

> 'A man who divorces his wife and marries another woman commits adultery against his wife. In the same way, a woman who divorces her husband and marries another man commits adultery'
> (Mark 10:11)

Divorce, remarriage and annulment
The law

Roman Catholic teaching on divorce and remarriage

The Church believes that Jesus was laying down a rule for his followers to obey, and that vows made in the name of God cannot be dissolved. **Divorce** is a 'grave offence' (Catechism of the Catholic Church) but it supports those who do get divorced.

Remarriage after divorce makes matters even worse, and those who remarry after divorce may not receive the Eucharist. They are, however, encouraged to attend Mass, as in other ways they often keep the faith and want to bring up their children as Christians.

On rare occasions, the Roman Catholic Church may grant an **annulment**, e.g. if it can be shown that one of the partners was forced into the marriage, suffered from mental problems at the time, never intended to keep the vows or was not baptised at the time of the marriage. An annulment is a declaration that a true marriage never took place. This means that the partners are free to 'remarry'.

Jesus' teaching on divorce and remarriage

Jesus taught that marriage was intended by God to be lifelong, and that the law permitting divorce was a concession to human weakness. In marriage the two became one. They were united by God and humans should not interfere with this.

Jesus' teaching about remarriage is recorded in two Gospels. According to Mark, Jesus said that remarriage after divorce was tantamount to adultery. According to Matthew, however, Jesus accepted remarriage after divorce if one partner had been unfaithful.

Protestant teaching on divorce

Attitudes vary in the Church of England.

- Some priests take the Roman Catholic view.

- Others will not allow remarriage in church on the grounds that the vows cannot be made twice, but they offer a service of marriage blessing after a civil marriage ceremony.

- Other priests adopt the attitude of the other Protestant churches. They believe that marriage is intended to be lifelong, but that people are human and make mistakes. They think Jesus' teaching was an ideal rather than a law, and they point out that he was always willing to give people a second chance and a fresh start. So they will allow the remarriage in church of people who have been divorced.

Prince Charles and Camilla Parker Bowles had a civil ceremony followed by a marriage blessing in St George's Chapel, Windsor

'Therefore what God has joined together, let no one separate' (Mark 10:9)

TopFoto

The importance of family and the elderly

- Commitment and responsibility are at the heart of family life.
- Parents to give children love, stability and Christian upbringing.
- Children to honour and respect parents (Ten Commandments) throughout their lives.
- Elderly to be shown love and respect and to be cared for appropriately to their needs.

> 'Each of you men should know how to live with his wife in a holy and honourable way, not with a lustful desire…'
> (1 Thessalonians 4:4–5)

> 'Children, it is your Christian duty to obey your parents always…Parents, do not irritate your children, or they will become discouraged'
> (Colossians 3:20–21)

> 'Respect your father and your mother'
> (Exodus 20:12)

> Jesus 'took the children in his arms, placed his hands on each of them, and blessed them'
> (Mark 10:16)

Key words

annulment
civil ceremony
civil partnership
cohabitation
divorce
religious ceremony
remarriage
sacramental covenant
vows

Test yourself

1 True or false?

TRUE FALSE

Marriage is a legal contract.

A civil ceremony may take place in a church.

A civil partnership is marriage between same-sex couples.

Civil partnerships give same-sex couples legal rights.

Cohabitation does not give couples legal rights.

A wedding ring symbolises unending love and faithfulness.

Jesus believed that marriage is intended to be for life.

Remarriage after divorce is never allowed by the Roman Catholic Church.

Remarriage after divorce is never allowed by the Church of England.

An annulment is a statement that a true marriage never took place.

2 Fill in the chart with six reasons why marriages sometimes break down.

```
                    ┌──────────────────┐
                    │                  │
                    │                  │
                    └──────────────────┘
                            ↓
┌──────────────────┐              ┌──────────────────┐
│                  │              │                  │
│                  │              │                  │
└──────────────────┘   ┌──────────────────┐   └──────────────────┘
          →            │  Why marriages   │            ←
          →            │   break down     │            ←
┌──────────────────┐   └──────────────────┘   ┌──────────────────┐
│                  │            ↑              │                  │
│                  │                           │                  │
└──────────────────┘                          └──────────────────┘
                    ┌──────────────────┐
                    │                  │
                    │                  │
                    └──────────────────┘
```

'Wives must submit completely to their husbands just as the church submits itself to Christ…Husbands, love your wives just as Christ loved the church and gave his life for it…every husband must love his wife as himself, and every wife must respect her husband' (Ephesians 5:24,25,33)

Examination question

a Describe support that might be given to couples who are experiencing marriage problems. *(4 marks)*

Exam tip

Remember to look carefully at the trigger word. If it says 'describe', you do not need to give any explanation. You would not lose marks for doing so, but you would not gain any, so you would penalise yourself by losing valuable time.

b 'Remarriage in church after a divorce should never be allowed.'

What do you think? Explain your opinion. *(3 marks)*

Prejudice and discrimination

Prejudice

Prejudice refers to what goes on in the mind. It consists of pre-judging, i.e. holding fixed views on someone or something without good reason. Prejudiced views are irrational, e.g. thinking that all women are bad car drivers.

'I recommend to you our sister Phoebe, who serves the church… Receive her in the Lord's name, as God's people should…'
(Romans 16:1)

Discrimination

Discrimination is putting prejudice into action. It is treating someone in a particular way (usually negatively) without good reason, e.g. refusing to employ someone as a taxi driver because she is a woman.

Causes of prejudice and discrimination

There are many reasons. The fundamental cause is ignorance. Lack of knowledge and understanding underlies most prejudice.

'From one man he made all the nations…'
(Acts 17:26)

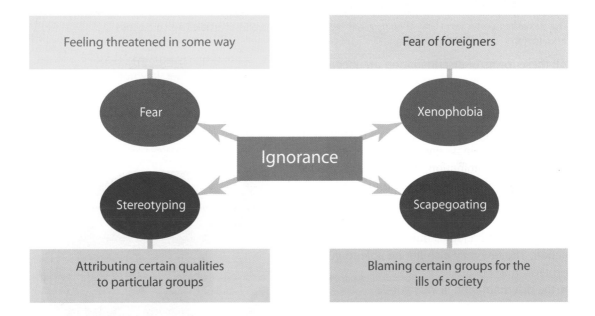

Types of prejudice and discrimination

You have to know about four types:

- colour and racial — particularly towards black people
- religious — often towards Muslims
- gender — usually towards women
- disability — towards both mentally and physically disabled people

'…love your neighbour as you love yourself'
(Leviticus 19:18)

The success of Dame Tanni Grey-Thompson has helped raise the profile of athletes with disabilities

All these forms of discrimination are illegal. The law covers many areas, e.g. employment, education, benefits, housing. It also deals with verbal discrimination, for example, the kind of speech that might encourage racial hatred, verbal harassment of female employees by employers. Victims of discrimination can take their case to tribunal. But discrimination continues to be a major problem in the UK because the law cannot dictate how people think. It cannot prosecute prejudice, and prejudice quickly spills over into action. The law may also not be able to give protection if:

- the discrimination is very subtle
- there are no witnesses
- witnesses are afraid to give evidence
- the victim does not report anything for fear of what will follow
- the victim is not as articulate or well represented legally as the discriminator
- there is **institutional racism** as, for example, was seen to be the case in the Stephen Lawrence murder investigation

'There is neither Jew nor Gentile, neither slave nor free, neither male nor female, for you are all one in Christ Jesus' (Galatians 3:27)

Stephen Lawrence

Christian views on prejudice and discrimination

All Christians agree that prejudice and discrimination are sinful. The Bible makes it clear that all people are children of God, to be treated with the respect and dignity that their status as human beings deserves. In the past, Christians have been guilty of all four types of discrimination, but the Church has long recognised that this is incompatible with the teaching of the New Testament in particular. Jesus treated everyone equally and fairly: he healed both Jews and Gentiles, men and women and the disabled. He told a story in which an injured Jew was ignored by fellow countrymen whose status as religious leaders meant they should have known better. It was a Samaritan, whose people and the Jews were bitter enemies, who stopped to help him. In all the Gospel accounts women were the first to be told of Jesus' resurrection. Like Jesus, Christians believe in **equality**, i.e. that all human beings have equal value and should be treated the same. They also believe in **justice**, i.e. that all human beings have the same right to fair and equal treatment.

By word: in sermons and speeches, by refusing to join in racist conversation

How can religious believers counter prejudice and discrimination?

By action: protest marches, writing to MPs, befriending vulnerable groups

By example: parents and other adults setting a good example

 Case study

Martin Luther King Jr

- Born in the USA in 1929 — a black American
- Became a Baptist minister and the leader of the black community in his town
- Led the bus boycott in 1955 after Rosa Parkes was arrested for refusing to give up her seat on the bus to a white man, and this resulted in desegregation of buses
- Became leader of the civil rights movement — involved in a wide variety of non-violent protests that led gradually to desegregation of schools, restaurants etc.
- Despite threats to his life and a bomb left outside his house, he constantly advocated non-violence — the only way to neutralise evil was by responding to it with love
- Gave the 'I have a dream' speech at a huge rally in Washington, speaking of his dream that one day all races, religions etc. would live together in harmony
- Awarded the Nobel Peace Prize in 1964
- Black people given the vote in 1965
- Assassinated in 1968

Key words

discrimination
equality
institutional racism
justice
prejudice
scapegoating
stereotyping
xenophobia

Test yourself

1 Name two causes of prejudice.

2 Name two forms of discrimination.

3 'For Christians, discrimination is the greatest moral evil.'
What do you think? Explain your opinion.

B I don't want to employ a woman — the men working under her won't like it.

Examination question

A Sorry, you can't have the job. I don't think it's suitable for a woman, so I'd prefer to appoint a man.

Exam tip

If stimulus material is given at the start of a question, do look at it carefully and make good use of it in the exam question. It is not just decoration or included to fill in a space.

a **Which is an example of prejudice: A or B?** *(1 mark)*

b **Which is an example of discrimination: A or B?** *(1 mark)*

c **What is the difference between prejudice and discrimination?** *(2 marks)*

d **Explain Christian attitudes to prejudice and discrimination.** *(6 marks)*

Topic 5
Global concerns

The environment

- Acid rain
- Destruction of rainforests
- Extinction of species
- Thinning ozone layer
- Environmental problems
- River/lake pollution
- Greenhouse gases
- Sea pollution
- Pesticides
- Toxic waste

Global warming is intensifying droughts

TopFoto

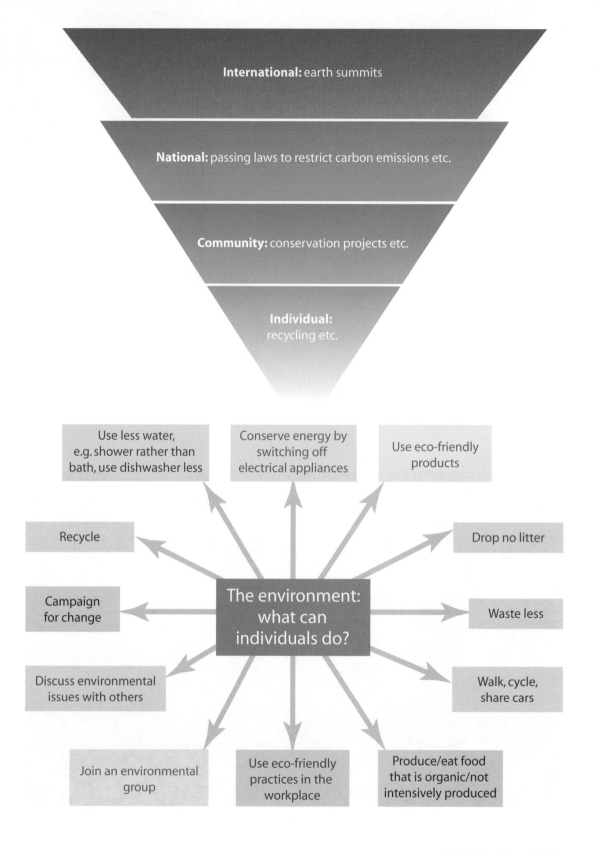

International: earth summits

National: passing laws to restrict carbon emissions etc.

Community: conservation projects etc.

Individual:
recycling etc.

Use less water,
e.g. shower rather than
bath, use dishwasher less

Conserve energy by
switching off
electrical appliances

Use eco-friendly
products

Recycle

Drop no litter

Campaign
for change

The environment:
what can
individuals do?

Waste less

Discuss environmental
issues with others

Walk, cycle,
share cars

Join an environmental
group

Use eco-friendly
practices in the
workplace

Produce/eat food
that is organic/not
intensively produced

Christian attitudes to the environment

Christians attend services to thank God for the harvest

- Stewardship entails the recognition that humans do not own the world but are entrusted by God with its care; this means maintaining the world as God would wish, and also taking into account the needs of those in LEDCs.

- Justice entails fair treatment, i.e. humans have to conserve the world and those living in the developed world have a duty to use its resources wisely, with the interests and rights of both those in LEDCs and future generations in mind.

- Respect for life means recognising that everyone and everything in the world is part of God's creation, valued by him and to be treated accordingly.

- Christians acknowledge God as the Creator in Harvest Festival services.

- Humans have great power, which must be used responsibly.

- The concept of sanctity of life extends beyond humans.

- Many churches are becoming **eco-friendly**, with strict policies on use of energy for example.

- Major aid agencies are involved with environmental issues because of the link with global poverty, and there are many Christian environmental agencies, e.g. **A Rocha**.

- In 1986 Christian leaders of all denominations issued a set of statements that formed part of the **Assisi Declarations** on beliefs about the earth and commitment to environmental conservation; these were issued; they met with leaders from other faiths at Assisi, the birthplace of **St Francis of Assisi** (patron saint of animals).

'Then God said, "And now we will make human beings; they will be like us…They will have power over…all animals…" He created them…and said, "…I am putting you in charge of…all the wild animals"'
(Genesis 1:26–28)

'Lord, you have made so many things! How wisely you made them all! The earth is filled with your creatures'
(Psalm 104:24)

'God looked at everything he had made, and he was very pleased'
(Genesis 1:31)

'Look at the birds: they do not sow seeds, gather a harvest and put it in barns; yet your Father in heaven takes care of them!'
(Matthew 6:26)

'Then the Lord God placed the man in the Garden of Eden to cultivate it and guard it'
(Genesis 2:15)

A ROCHA

Caring for God's world together

- Christian conservation organisation
- Started in Portugal in 1983 — the word means 'the rock'
- Now spread to five continents
- Has projects in 18 countries and takes on volunteer workers
- Concerned with conservation and saving species from extinction
- Building up of eco-tourist industry in Kenya has led to better provision of secondary education in its coastal region

Key words

A Rocha
acid rain
Assisi Declarations
conservation
earth summits
eco-friendly
extinction
pollution
recycling
St Francis of Assisi

Test yourself

1 Fill in the gaps in the chart below:

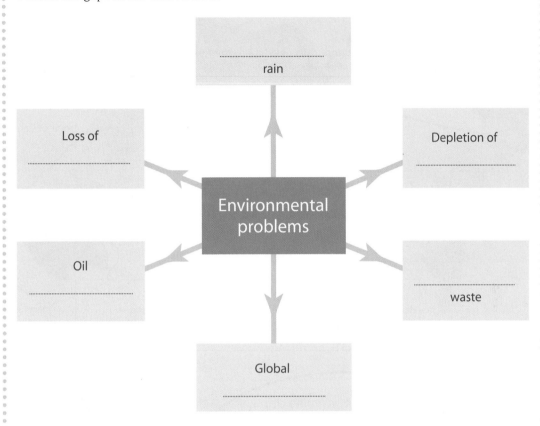

rain

Loss of
....

Depletion of
....

Oil
....

Environmental problems

waste

Global
....

2 What forms of international action are being taken to conserve the world?

3 What can the UK government do to conserve resources?

4 How can local communities be involved in conservation?

Examination question

a **Explain how individual Christians might be involved in conserving the environment.** *(6 marks)*

b **Explain why Christians believe it is important to conserve the environment.** *(6 marks)*

Exam tip

Read the question very carefully. If the trigger word is 'explain', note whether it is a 'how' or 'why' question. Many marks are lost in exams through candidates explaining how, when they are required to explain why, and vice versa.

World poverty

More economically developed countries

Brandt Line

Tropic of Cancer

Equator

Less economically developed countries

Tropic of Capricorn

	Human development index	
Most developed ←		→ Least developed

0.9–1.0　0.8–0.89　0.7–0.79　0.6–0.69　0.5–0.59　<0.5　N/A

Hi! I'm Liz. I'm 13 and I live in the UK. I go to the local comp, which is only a mile down the road, but my mum takes me in the car every day, so I don't have to get up early. I love weekends, as then I go down to town with my friends — we sometimes buy DVDs or clothes if our mums are feeling generous, and we always go for a burger. I hope to go to uni and then work in a big law firm.

Hi! I'm Grace. I'm 13 and I live in Uganda. My parents both died of AIDS when I was little and I hardly remember them. Luckily, my aunt said she would look after me even though she's a widow, so I live with her and my three young cousins. But we don't have enough money for me to go to school so I help her with the animals. I also fetch water and sometimes prepare the meal that we have once a day. I'd love to become a teacher, but that is just a dream — I can't read or write.

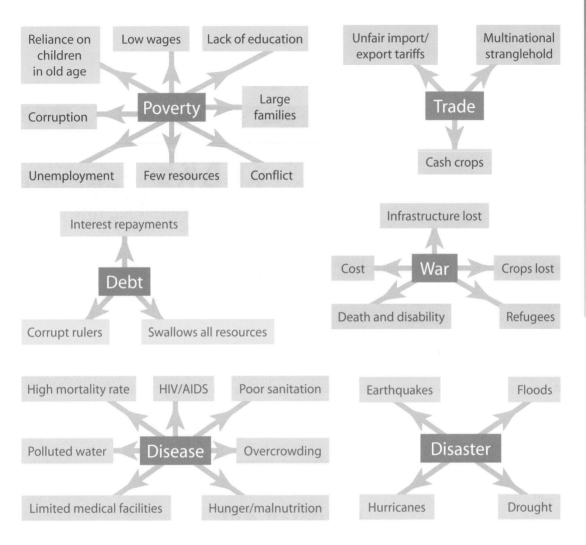

Response to global poverty

A small percentage of the UK's national income is given annually to projects in less economically developed countries (LEDCs) to help reduce poverty. In an emergency, e.g. the 2004 Asian tsunami, large sums are given for immediate relief. But much of the response comes from charities.

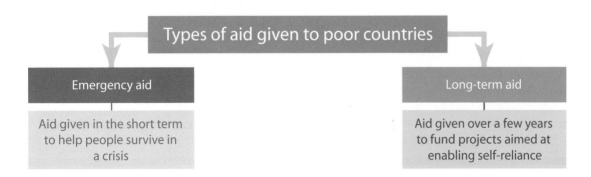

CAFOD

- Began with first Family Fast Day in 1960 organised by National Board of Catholic Women
- Set up by Catholic Bishops of England and Wales in 1962 as official overseas development and relief agency
- Works with over 500 partners in the UK and overseas
- Also works with other UK agencies, e.g. Disasters Emergency Committee, and with interfaith groups, e.g. Islamic Relief

CAFOD activists lobbying parliament to make poverty history

- Helped to set up **fair trade** movement
- Basic principles — compassion, solidarity, stewardship, hope
- Concerned to promote human development and social justice
- Involved in emergency and long-term aid, in encouraging a more simple lifestyle in the UK and in speaking out against injustice

 Case study

Christian Aid

- Started as agency to help refugees in Europe at end of Second World War
- Committed to seeing a just world now, not just in the future — one of its slogans
- Belief in life before death — another of its slogans
- Works on development projects with partner organisations in countries all over the world
- Involved in both emergency and long-term aid
- Also works with other UK agencies
- Founder member of fair trade movement
- Involved in many campaigns to get rid of debt, unfair trade, war etc.
- Annual Christian Aid week — envelopes put through as many UK letterboxes as possible and then collected by volunteers

Case study

Tearfund

- A Christian organisation born out of the Evangelical Alliance in 1968
- Involved in five main areas:
  - HIV
  - health, sanitation, education etc.
  - environmental issues
  - challenging injustice
  - tackling disasters
- Works in 64 countries through 500 church-based partner organisations
- Runs Tearcraft, a fair trade organisation that works through 19 partners
- 10-year vision — release of 50 million people from physical and spiritual hunger through network of 100,000 local churches

Case study

Trócaire

- Set up by the Irish Catholic bishops in 1973 as the official overseas development agency of the Catholic Church in Ireland
- Means 'mercy' in English
- Works in 39 countries across Asia, Africa, Latin America and the Middle East
- Stresses the dignity, fundamental human rights and responsibilities of all people, regardless of race, creed, culture etc.
- Raises awareness about root causes of poverty and injustice and encourages action
- Involved in emergency and long-term aid

Fair trade

This movement was started by a number of aid agencies and organisations. Fair trade aims at removing the injustice at the heart of much world trade, e.g. those who work on banana plantations for multinational companies are very poorly paid. Fair trade aims to give the producers of goods a fair wage for their goods. Those involved in the movement also aim to provide decent living and working conditions for the workers, including schools for children and medical care. They encourage the setting up of cooperatives and the using of suitable technology.

Fair trade is about better prices, decent working conditions, local sustainability and fair terms of trade for farmers and workers in the developing world

Christian attitudes to world poverty

- All mainstream Christian denominations take an active part in working towards ending global poverty.

- They emphasise:
  - justice
  - stewardship
  - compassion
  - following the example of Jesus

- When they help the poor, they are reminded of what Jesus said in the parable of the sheep and goats, that whatever a person did for someone else, whoever it was and however basic the act of kindness, it was done to Jesus.

- They follow New Testament teaching that it is not enough to say that poverty is wrong; action is needed, and that a person who ignores someone in need cannot possibly claim to love God (1 John 3:17–18).

- Christians are called to give generously and self-sacrificially of their money, their time and their talents.

- The Christian churches teach that rich nations have a moral duty to help poor nations, both by giving direct aid and by reforming those international agencies (e.g. the World Trade Organization) that keep poor nations poor.

- Many Christians give up luxuries in Lent, take part in fast days and Lenten lunches, and in sponsored activities.

- Many also take part in campaigns such as Make Poverty History.

'One of them, named Agabus…predicted that a severe famine was about to come over all the earth…The disciples decided that each of them would send as much as he could to help…'
(Acts 11:28–29)

'Each one should give…not with regret or out of a sense of duty; for God loves the one who gives gladly'
(2 Corinthians 9:7)

'I was hungry and you fed me, thirsty and you gave me a drink…Whenever you did this for one of the least important of these brothers of mine, you did it for me!'
(Matthew 25:35,40)

'The whole group of those who believed were of one heart and soul, and no one claimed private ownership of any possessions, but everything they owned was held in common'
(Acts 4:32)

'If any one of you has material possessions and sees a brother or sister in need but has no pity on them, how can the love of God be in you? Dear children, let us not love with words or tongue but with actions and in truth'
(1 John 3:17–18)

Test yourself

1 Give six facts about CAFOD, Christian Aid, Tearfund or Trócaire in the chart below:

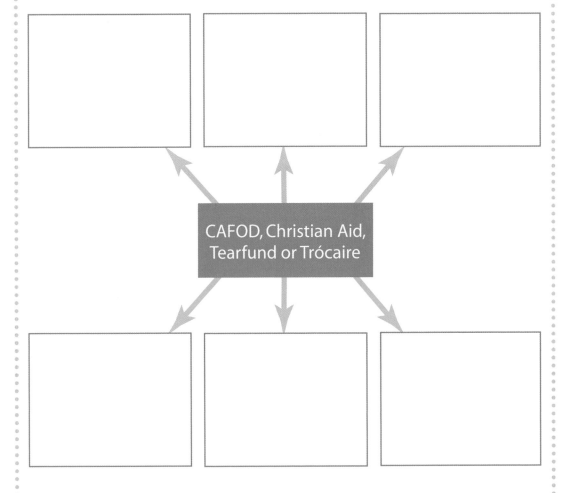

CAFOD, Christian Aid, Tearfund or Trócaire

2 Explain the difference between emergency and long-term aid.

Examination question

Do you like my new skirt and top? I went to that big store on the high street and I was really lucky. My mum gave me some money to treat myself, and because they were so cheap, I had enough to go and buy some earrings that I've been wanting for ages. I really couldn't believe how cheap they were — I got a real bargain. And they were made in India — so I feel as if I've been helping the poor.

You must be joking. That store was on the news last week — an undercover reporter had discovered that those who make clothes for it are really exploited — they work long hours in awful conditions for almost nothing. If you really want to help the poor, be more careful where you shop.

a Explain briefly how the Fair trade movement seeks to help workers in poor nations.

(3 marks)

Exam tip

You are required to know about the work of one of the listed voluntary aid agencies. Make sure you keep to one of those on the list and learn several aspects of its work.

b 'If people have poor working conditions, their own governments should sort it out. It's not our concern.'

Do you agree? Give reasons for your answer, showing that you have thought about more than one point of view. Refer to Christian teaching in your answer.

(6 marks)

Topic 6
Conflict

War and peace

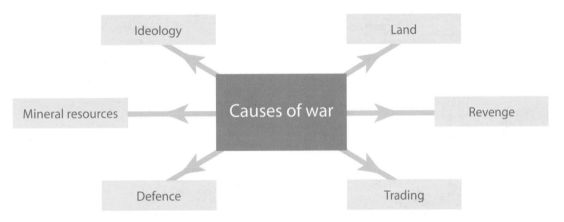

Causes of war

- Ideology
- Land
- Mineral resources
- Revenge
- Defence
- Trading

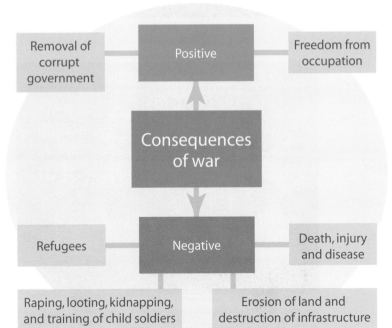

Consequences of war

Positive
- Removal of corrupt government
- Freedom from occupation

Negative
- Refugees
- Death, injury and disease
- Raping, looting, kidnapping, and training of child soldiers
- Erosion of land and destruction of infrastructure

TopFoto

One result of war is that many people have to flee from their homes

Types of warfare

Conventional warfare covers a wide range of weaponry, including:

- atomic (nuclear)
- biological
- chemical

The first example of **nuclear warfare** was in August 1945 when the USA dropped atomic bombs on Hiroshima and Nagasaki in Japan. Thousands died immediately and many more thousands died slowly from the effects of radiation. Still today, people are dying of cancers related to the dropping of those bombs.

The atomic bomb dropped on Hiroshima completely destroyed the city

Many nations, including the UK, have nuclear weapons. They see them as a deterrent: possession of them protects them from attack. Some other nations are in the process of developing nuclear technology, and this is a cause of concern. **Nuclear proliferation** might lead to irresponsible leaders or terrorists getting hold of such weapons and using them. Some Christians join CND, which is an organisation that campaigns to get rid of nuclear weapons in all countries, including the UK.

Protesters campaigning for nuclear disarmament

Terrorism

This is the often indiscriminate use of violence to achieve particular political or religious goals, to redress injustice or to overthrow a regime. Whatever the motive, **terrorism** is aimed at creating an atmosphere of fear and putting pressure on those in power. A common form of terrorism is suicide bombing, and those who die in this way are regarded as martyrs. Terrorists justify their actions as a last resort: they are seen as the only way of making people listen to their grievances. Most people, however, condemn all acts of terrorism, claiming that they show a total disregard for life and can never be justified.

The Just War theory

The **Just War theory** refers to the belief that war is never a good thing, but sometimes it may be justified as the lesser of two evils. It is a very ancient theory, but was developed over the centuries by great thinkers in the Roman Catholic Church. Some politicians and journalists use it when assessing whether or not conflict is justified. For a war to be declared just, eight criteria are taken into account.

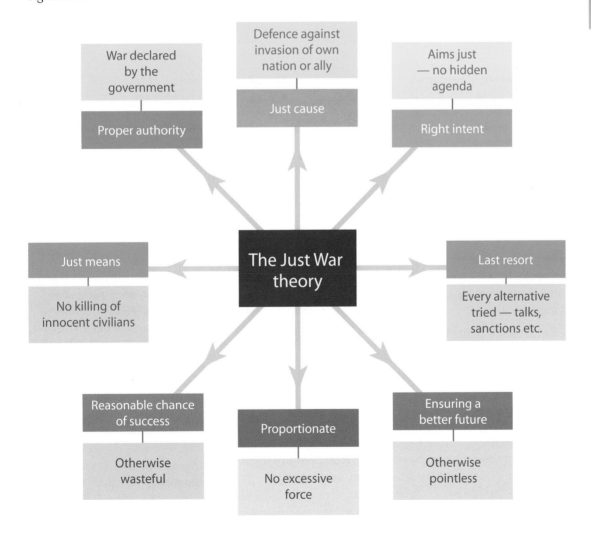

Pacifism

This is the belief that violence against other human beings can never be justified. War is always wrong: it can never be the lesser of two evils. There are strong arguments both for and against **pacifism**.

Arguments for pacifism	Arguments against pacifism
Beliefs about human life ■ everyone has the right to life ■ life is sacred ■ lives should be treated with respect ■ all are brothers and sisters	**The right to life is not absolute** ■ an aggressor has forfeited that right by the act of aggression ■ some lives may be sacrificed to protect others
War causes immense suffering ■ modern methods in particular harm the innocent ■ the suffering caused is out of all proportion to the evil being fought ■ the emotional suffering may affect future generations	**The Just War conditions** ■ seek to protect the innocent ■ ensure proportionality in violence ■ refusal to fight may make aggressors think they can do whatever they want, which may result in more suffering. It is important to defend and protect the innocent and sometimes this can be done only through war
War is a waste of resources ■ the money spent in the UK on weapons would solve social and global problems ■ money should be spent on saving lives, not destroying them ■ it causes irreparable damage to the environment ■ it uses up minerals and other resources	**War can be a wise use of resources** ■ wars that are fought to end injustice may save money and resources in the long run as greedy oppressors waste resources even more
War encourages undesirable attitudes ■ e.g. greed, hatred, prejudice, lust for power, arrogance	**War brings out the best in people** ■ e.g. courage, comradeship, compassion, humility, desire for justice

'Happy are those who work for peace; God will call them his children!' (Matthew 5:9)

'Forgive us the wrongs we have done, as we forgive the wrongs that others have done to us' (Matthew 6:12)

'Everyone must obey the state authorities, because no authority exists without God's permission' (Romans 13:1)

'...love your enemies and pray for those who persecute you' (Matthew 5:44)

'"Put your sword back in its place," Jesus said to him. "All who take the sword will die by the sword."' (Matthew 26:52)

'When they came to the place called "The Skull", they crucified Jesus there...Jesus said, "Forgive them, Father! They don't know what they are doing."' (Luke 23:33–34)

Christian attitudes to war and peace

- All Christians stress the importance of **reconciliation**, **forgiveness**, justice and **peace**.

- The different views of Christians do not coincide with differences in denominations, i.e. some Roman Catholics, Anglicans and Methodists are pacifist and some are not.

- The Society of Friends (Quakers) is the only denomination that is officially pacifist.

- There are many Christian pacifist groups, e.g. Pax Christi.

- Christian pacifists refer to the teaching of Jesus
  - love your enemies and pray for your persecutors
  - those who live by the sword die by the sword

- Christians who are not pacifist tend to agree with the approach of the Just War theory.

- They claim that the teaching and example of Jesus were unrelated to issues of war and peace and should not be taken literally or distorted.

- St Paul told Christians to obey rulers because they were given their authority from God.

- The Catechism of the Catholic Church supports the Just War theory, accepting that war may occasionally be a 'necessary evil'.

- Pope John XXIII spoke out against nuclear weapons in 1963.

 Case study

Cross of Nails centres

- In 1940 Coventry cathedral (along with much of Coventry) was destroyed by German bombs
- The Provost wrote the words 'Father forgive' on the sanctuary wall; two charred beams that had fallen in the shape of a cross were set up on the altar and three of the medieval nails were bound together in the shape of a cross
- Crosses of Nails became a symbol of reconciliation and peace
- At the end of the war, Crosses of Nails were sent to German cities bombed by the Allies
- There are now 160 Cross of Nails centres throughout the world, working for reconciliation and peace, e.g. in the Middle East (working with Jews and Arabs) and in South Africa (healing the terrible memories of apartheid)

Dietrich Bonhoeffer

Statue of Dietrich Bonhoeffer who was commemorated as a martyr, Westminster Abbey

- Born in Germany in 1906
- Protestant Christian
- Studied theology and became a Lutheran pastor
- Co-founded the Confessing Church — which opposed Hitler and the Nazis
- Helped Jews escape from Germany
- Rejected earlier pacifist views because he believed that the evil of Nazism could be overcome only by violence
- Plotted overthrow of Hitler
- Arrested and eventually moved to Flossenburg concentration camp
- Hanged in April 1945
- Commemorated as a martyr by the Church of England

Key words

- forgiveness
- nuclear proliferation
- nuclear warfare
- pacifism
- peace
- reconciliation
- terrorism
- Just War theory

Test yourself

1 Read through the following statements relating to the Second World War. Next to each, say which criterion of the Just War theory could be applied and then put a tick or cross, indicating whether you think it was fulfilled or not. The first has been done for you as an example.

The UK went to war with Germany because Hitler invaded Poland, with whom the UK had an alliance	*Just cause*	✓
The British government declared war on Germany		
Before declaring war, Britain had held talks with Hitler and made a treaty — but Hitler ignored it		
Britain had an army, a navy and an air force that were reasonably equipped		
Europe suffered terribly under Nazi rule. After the war, Eastern Europe was dominated by the Soviet Union and its repressive policies		
Thousands of civilians died in the bombing of Dresden by the RAF and allies		
The Americans dropped nuclear bombs on Hiroshima and Nagasaki		
When Germany surrendered, the British and Americans began to help German refugees		

2 Give three reasons why pacifists did not agree with the UK going to war against Germany in 1939.

3 Explain briefly two consequences of war.

Examination question

a 'Christians who fight in a war are betraying their faith.'

What do you think? Explain your opinion. *(3 marks)*

Exam tip

When explaining views, you may find it helpful in developing your answer to give examples of people or organisations that hold those views.

b **Explain why many Christians are pacifists.** *(6 marks)*

c **Explain why many Christians support the Just War theory.** *(6 marks)*

Crime and punishment

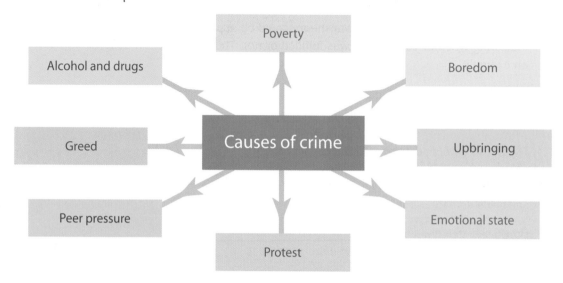

Poverty

Alcohol and drugs

Boredom

Greed

Causes of crime

Upbringing

Peer pressure

Emotional state

Protest

Forms of punishment

There are many different types of punishment that a judge or magistrate can give an offender. When deciding on a sentence, the offender's past history is taken into account, along with any mitigating circumstances and the seriousness of the offence.

Imprisonment

- There are four categories of adult **prison**, ranging from high security for offenders who might pose a threat to society (category A) to open prisons for those nearing the end of a sentence or who are not dangerous.
- The conditions in many prisons are very bad:
  - overcrowding and poor sanitation
  - lack of opportunity for education and work training
  - bullying
  - being locked up for almost the whole day
- Young people who need to be kept in custody may be put in:
  - young offender institutions
  - secure training centres
  - local authority secure children's homes
- Adult prisoners who have behaved well in prison, who show signs of remorse and who are unlikely to pose a threat to society may be given parole, which involves early release with monitoring by a parole officer and sometimes electronic tagging.

Imprisonment is just one type of punishment that can be given to offenders

Probation
Offenders are under the supervision of a **probation** officer for a set period of time. They meet up regularly to discuss progress.

Community service
Offenders have to carry out unpaid work that benefits the community in their own time for a set period of hours.

Fines
These are sums of money paid to the court and are used for a variety of offences.

Electronic tagging and curfews
These are intended to enable the police to monitor the whereabouts of offenders and restrict their movements.

ASBOs
These prevent individuals from being in an area where they have caused problems for the community in the past.

Aims of punishment
Magistrates and judges give sentences that are intended to achieve particular aims. You need to know about four aims of punishment (though there are more). Increasingly the authorities are interested in **restorative justice**.

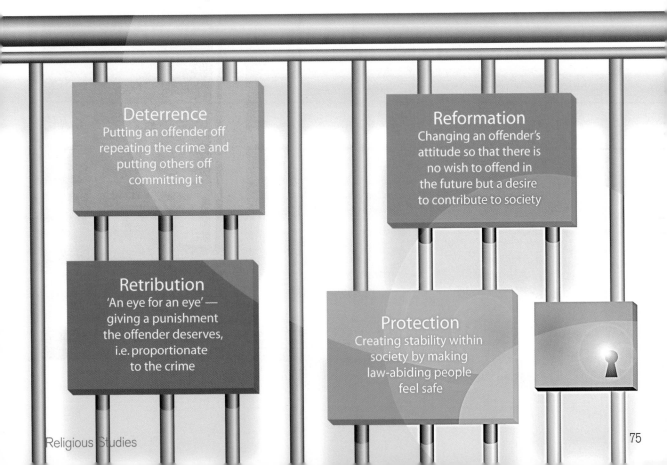

Deterrence
Putting an offender off repeating the crime and putting others off committing it

Reformation
Changing an offender's attitude so that there is no wish to offend in the future but a desire to contribute to society

Retribution
'An eye for an eye' — giving a punishment the offender deserves, i.e. proportionate to the crime

Protection
Creating stability within society by making law-abiding people feel safe

Christian attitudes to crime and punishment

Christians believe that the law gives stability to society and should always be obeyed, unless it conflicts with God's will as revealed in the Bible, the teachings of the Church and conscience. Jesus said: 'Give to Caesar what belongs to him and to God what belongs to him.' So Christians accept that punishment may be needed to ensure that justice is carried out and to enable offenders to recognise the hurt they have caused and come to terms with it. But punishment should always go hand in hand with forgiveness; offenders should always have the chance to make a fresh start and victims should be helped to move on and not be consumed by bitterness and the desire for revenge. So for most Christians, reformation is the most important aim of punishment.

A recently released prisoner trying on clothes donated by a church

The Church also gives practical help to offenders who want to make a fresh start. Prisons have chaplains to celebrate Mass and other sacraments and to give support. The SVP helps offenders and their families, and some Christian employers are willing to give ex-offenders a job.

Reformation

Restorative justice: offenders make amends to their victims (e.g. repairing damage) or meet their victims to talk things through

Education: offenders learn literacy skills, take exams, train in vocational skills

Gives offenders a second chance and victims and society a chance to forgive and move on

Those in prison contribute positively to society instead of feeling cut off from it

Jesus said: 'Love your enemies and pray for those who persecute you'

Example: learning Braille and transcribing books for blind people

'Forgive us our sins, as we forgive those who have sinned against us'

Example: the Dartmoor Storybook Dads project helps fathers and their children

Prisoners working in an upholstery workshop at HM Prison Manchester

Christian views about the death penalty (capital punishment)

Many countries still carry the **death penalty** out for serious offences, e.g. the USA, but in the UK it was abolished 50 years ago. Some Christians would like it to be restored, putting forward a number of arguments for it.

The Catechism of the Catholic Church allows for the death penalty in very serious cases, where it seems the only appropriate response to a terrible crime, but at the same time states its preference for 'bloodless solutions', and Pope John Paul II was opposed to it.

Many other denominations, e.g. Anglican and Quaker, have made official statements opposing it, and most Christians take this position.

 Case study

Sister Helen Prejean, CSV

- Born in Louisiana in 1939 and became a nun in 1957
- Became involved in prison work in 1981
- Became the pen pal of a man on Death Row in Louisiana
- Visited him, became his spiritual advisor and was with him as he went to the electric chair
- Seeing what life was like on Death Row and witnessing his death led to her becoming a prominent campaigner against the death penalty
- She also founded Survive, an organisation that provides counselling for the families of victims of violence
- She sees two rights as absolutely fundamental: the right not to be tortured and the right not to be killed
- She believes in the teaching of Jesus not to reply to hate with hate

Sister Helen Prejean

'When they came to the place called "The Skull", they crucified Jesus there…Jesus said, "Forgive them, Father! They don't know what they are doing."'
(Luke 23:33–34)

'You have heard that it was said, "An eye for an eye and a tooth for a tooth." But I say to you: do not resist an evildoer. But if anyone strikes you on the right cheek, turn the other also'
(Matthew 5:38–39)

For the death penalty	Against the death penalty
Justice — 'an eye for an eye' — a murderer forfeits his or her own life	The 'eye for an eye' mentality encourages revenge, which is a negative and harmful attitude. Jesus asked God to forgive those who had nailed him to the cross
It shows love for the victims of serious crime	It does not show love for one's neighbour or for enemies
A second chance is not deserved — the victim doesn't have one	The offender has no chance to reform, to make a fresh start and become a useful citizen
The woman referred to in the column opposite had committed adultery, not murder. Maybe Jesus' verdict on a murderer would have been different	When Jesus was asked to pass sentence on a woman caught in the act of adultery (a capital offence in first-century Israel), he said those without sin should cast the first stone. He told her that he did not condemn her; she should go but not repeat her sin. He gave her a second chance
It provides absolute protection for society	Many murderers are not a danger to society as a whole and, if they are released, it is release on licence
It is the most effective deterrent	Evidence from the USA shows that it does not work as a deterrent
Forensic science makes wrongful execution more unlikely	Innocent people have been executed
The families of the victim never recover from their trauma — and they are innocent, too	It causes deep emotional and psychological trauma to the families of those executed — and the families are innocent

'...love your enemies and pray for those who persecute you' (Matthew 5:44)

'Jesus said, "I do not condemn you either. Go but do not sin again."' (John 8:11)

'Happy are those who work for peace; God will call them his children!' (Matthew 5:9)

'Everyone must obey the state authorities, because no authority exists without God's permission' (Romans 13:1)

'Forgive us the wrongs we have done, as we forgive the wrongs that others have done to us' (Matthew 6:12)

'Do not let evil defeat you; instead, conquer evil with good' (Romans 12:21)

Key words

ASBO
community service
death penalty
deterrence
electronic tagging
fines
prison
probation
protection
reformation
restorative justice
retribution

Test yourself

1 Explain briefly why people might commit crime.

2 Name one country that still carries out the death penalty.

3 Name one country that does not carry out the death penalty.

4 In the table below match up correctly each aim of punishment with its explanation.

Aim of punishment	Explanation of term
Deterrence	To compensate society/the victim in some way
Protection	To put the offender off committing crime again
Reformation	To give the offender what he/she deserves
Retribution	To keep society safe

Examination question

BREAKING NEWS! Inspector of prisons slams three prisons over appalling conditions for prisoners!

1 Outline the concerns that many people have about some prisons in the UK. *(4 marks)*

Exam tip

The command word 'outline' requires only a brief summary of the key points; a detailed description is not required.

2 'Convicted murderers should always receive the death penalty.' Do you agree? Give reasons for your answer, showing that you have thought about more than one point of view. Refer to Christian teachings in your answer. *(6 marks)*

abortion 6
acid rain 55
active euthanasia 13
addiction 41
adult stem cells 30
adultery 35
AID 19
AIH 19
annulment 47
A Rocha 57
ASBO 75
Assisi Declarations 57
autonomy 7
CAFOD 62
cannabis 41
chastity 35
Christian Aid 62
civil ceremony 44
civil partnership 45
cloning 28
cohabitation 45
community service 75
conception 7
conservation 56
contraception 34
death penalty 77
designer babies 23
deterrence 75
DI 19
discrimination 51
divorce 47
drug 42
earth summits 56
eco-friendly 57
electronic tagging 75
embryo 7
embryonic research 19
embryonic stem cells 30
emergency aid 61

equality 53
euthanasia 13
excommunication 10
extinction 55
Fair trade 63
fertility treatment 18
fines 75
foetus 7
forgiveness 71
gene therapy 23
genetic engineering 23
heterosexuality 33
HFEA 19
homosexuality 33
hybrid embryos 31
idolatry 27
infertility 18
institutional racism 52
involuntary euthanasia 13
IVF 19
justice 53
Just War theory 69
living wills 14
long-term aid 61
non-voluntary euthanasia 13
nuclear proliferation 68
nuclear warfare 68
pacifism 70
palliative care 15
passive euthanasia 13
peace 71
pollution 55
pre-implantation genetic
   diagnosis 25
prejudice 51
premarital sexual
   relationships 35
prison 74
probation 75

pro-choice 8
procreative 20
pro-life 8
protection 75
reconciliation 71
recycling 56
reformation 75
rehabilitation 41
religious ceremony 44
remarriage 47
reproductive cloning 29
restorative justice 75
retribution 75
sacramental covenant 44
sanctity of life 20
saviour siblings 23
scapegoating 51
secular 7
self-determination 15
sexuality 35
somatic cell therapy 23
St Francis of Assisi 57
stereotyping 51
stewardship 15
surrogacy 20
Tearfund 63
teetotal 41
Trócaire 63
terrorism 69
the hospice movement 15
therapeutic cloning 30
Trócaire 63
unitive 20
viability 8
voluntary euthanasia 13
vows 44
xenophobia 51